# TRIBE
# OF
# ONE

**Memoir by Koki Doktori**

Copyright © 2024

All Rights Reserved

ISBN:

# Dedication

*Dedicated to my mother, Kamar (Tamar).*

# Acknowledgment

*Priska Juschka, Lani Funk Doktori, and Dymah Paige, for helping me tell my story.*

*Marty, Heyers, and Andrea Gentl, for all the photography in the book, thank you.*

# Table of Contents

| | |
|---|---|
| Introduction | 1 |
| In the Beginning | 3 |
| Arriving | 9 |
| Allen Street | 14 |
| Susan the Welsh | 17 |
| The Edge of the Precipice | 24 |
| Dawn in the Occident | 29 |
| Accidental Presumptions | 32 |
| At the River of Babylon | 36 |
| At the Refugee Camp | 44 |
| The Final Farewell | 50 |
| Becoming a Soldier | 57 |
| The Case of Accidental Reality | 60 |
| The Mystery of the Promised Land | 64 |
| The Perils of a New Home | 68 |
| Internal Conflicts | 74 |
| The Trauma of War | 77 |
| Return From the Ashes | 80 |
| Looking Back | 83 |
| Early Seduction | 86 |
| Challenges and Confrontations | 92 |
| Pursuing a Compromise | 95 |
| From Guilt to Attention | 99 |
| Concept to Conceptual | 107 |

| | |
|---|---|
| Driving a Taxi | 113 |
| Meeting at Magoo's | 120 |
| Horace and Jaffa | 125 |
| Boyhood | 128 |
| SoHo (South of Houston) | 131 |
| An Architectural Revolution | 137 |
| Being Attracted to a New Reality | 140 |
| Jack Smith and his Cockroach | 144 |
| New Gallery New Location | 148 |
| Changing the Changes | 152 |
| I Think Therefore I Am | 156 |
| Anne – the French | 159 |
| The End of One | 169 |
| Epilogue | 174 |

# About the Author

Born in Iraq to a family of Jewish heritage, Koki's father was a theology scholar who supported himself and the family as a goldsmith apprentice by day. At night, he studied the human condition and gathered the family to tell stories, a treasured tradition in an era without electronic devices or entertainment.

Koki became a visual artist, adapting his own form of storytelling, painting his ideas, and reflecting on his childhood memories. He went on to become an acclaimed artist whose artwork has been shown in numerous galleries and museums across the US, Europe, and Israel. This book is inspired by Koki's desire to recall ever more vividly his childhood journey, having emigrated with his family to Israel from Iraq in 1949. After 20 years in Israel, Koki emigrated to New York City to continue his pursuit of the fine arts and continues to live and work in NYC.

Page Blank Intentionally

# Introduction

I was not born an artist, as many other artists claim to have been. I came to this world without the skills to do anything and without a passion for any particular thing. Like a small boat rocking at sea in search of the north star, I have been on this search, to find myself and a vocation I can excel at.

I could not succeed at intellectual pursuits without the prerequisite language skills, which I did not have the opportunity to develop. The power of intellectualism through language required a time and resource investment that I could not commit to. As I began to look inward in search of my talents and what I could master, I realized my advantage was in how I used my hands and the things I could craft. My lack of language skills in my mother tongue, Arabic, or the Hebrew I spoke in my adopted country, Israel, did not allow me to pursue professions that were rooted in mastering the language. My escape and savior was in the physical world, following my father's footsteps, a goldsmith by trade. Shaping the physical materials with my hands and mind was my opportunity to thrive.

# In the Beginning

I did not know where to begin my pursuit of the arts. I started by searching the available schools and felt that being an artist, or more specifically, a sculptor, was something I could master. It was not difficult to get acceptance into the sculpting department of the Tel Aviv Art School, as, prior to applying, I had created a few clay sculptures, which I presented to the school's acceptance jury. This was the first time that I created something that was a meaningful part of me that went on to be recognized and rewarded by other people.

## Tribe of One

I came to realize that to earn a living as an artist, I had to move on to a place where I could do my work with physical materials, expressing my personality through these creations. My ambition in that category seemed to give me a lot of confidence, which allowed me to finally claim my place as an artist. I tried to look at other artists 'work for inspiration to create my own vision. At school, I found myself drawn to soft and malleable materials and started making sculptures of geometric shapes. Later, as I was more drawn to using different materials, I started to experiment with those that had not been used before.

My newer work, after I moved to NYC in the 70s, was not only better in terms of mastering my own unique style but also as a personal expression. My earliest work was interesting as my painting became sculptural. Now, in NYC, I was coating studs with latex in many layers, with the drips and flow of the liquid preserved, peeling the dried shape from its mold and hanging it on the wall, all that goes into the basic module remaining apparent. The hanging determines the final form, as gravity and the elasticity of the latex are compromised. This kind of procedural rigor had an impact outside the broader visual impressions my work may have left. The halfway position basic shape my work occupied could be both cast and molded, solidified and hung up in an interim as if the moment of change lasted forever.

The non-specific, organic sensuality of my work contrasted with the coarseness of the drippings and graphite on paper could echo the woodcut metallic pigments. However, what was perhaps most striking about these pieces was the nonchalance of their placements, an act which I found attested to the latent eloquence of the work itself.

Since the Abstract Expressionists freed the surface of the canvas from its literal dimensions and pictorial stability, artists have experimented with new investigations to liberate spatial contingencies within a work of art. My work was within a genre where the projection of the canvas into sculptural form by means of three-dimensional materials was developed and refined until it described an altogether new media.

In my early experiments with latex, I delved into the problems presented by the overlap between maintaining a two-dimensional aspect with a three-dimensional form. I was most interested in molding the material so it underwent its greatest transformation, thereby pushing it to its outer limits. Throughout the various stages of my work, I had a strong respect for the innate two-dimensional gravitational character of the latex, all the while pressing it to full three-dimensional expression, ultimately driving a full evolution of the merging of the multi-dimensions of form and space.

Over time, I became more and more interested in painting. I was drawn to minimal art and the various permutations of structure, music, and performance. The art world was less involved with material objects and more given to a dematerialized aesthetic. The focus on time and process was indicative of a new conscious expansion in American culture. This, in turn, was combined with a reductive experimentation in music, art, theater, film, and dance.

My watercolors demonstrated a primacy of form, constituted of open shapes and distinguished by individual colors; they achieved a sculptural effect despite being two-dimensional. In my paintings, as in my sculptures, color subordinates itself to form. Graphite on paper can echo the woodcut. My works on paper are naturally small, and I have found that just as watercolors can evoke sculpture, small pieces can have monument-like effects or remind us of the quotidian experiences of a diary.

Coming from Israel, I felt an instinctive connection with the era's new structures in art. I interpreted them less as a Puritan mode of expression, which was often the case for American criticism, and more as a kind of ecstatic recognition of consciousness, an internal manifestation of time and space.

In the Middle East, the tradition of writing, the calligraphic stroke, functions as a continuum of life. Signs flow from one level of significance to another, a flow of language. To understand my work – the ecstatic writing –one cannot avoid the Middle Eastern context in which the flow of the language is felt. In grammatical terms, one may speak of my art as a conjugation of Arabic script and Judaic contemplation. In the best sense, it is an obsessive art form and is intent upon a desire to control the excess of language. In doing so, my paintings and calligraphic sketches embed a tradition of reductive thought where "less is more." In the tradition of writing, structure defines itself in relation to overall space. This idea has been appropriated in American Modernism, ranging from the architectural decorum of Louis Sullivan to the action painting of

# Tribe of One

Pollock. In my paintings, writing is contingent upon decoration. Decoration and writing are virtually synonymous. One cannot separate writing from ornament. It is both non-figurative and non-anthropomorphic.

Influenced early on by Structuralist music and related experimental forms, I adapted that language into a visual form that was inherently connected to my Middle Eastern traditions. My paintings have always been meditative, a search for tranquility amid the chaos of existence. I build and sculpt my art, carving it, working with knives, raising the material, lowering it, and cutting it. I enjoy the materiality and boldness of my works. The foundation of my art is connecting the compositional issues (i.e., modern music) and the referential issues (i.e., calligraphy). My fundamental concern was with the accumulation of lines in my paintings. What I appreciated in the work of modern composers, like Philip Glass, or Steve Reich, both of whom use one single tone in its repetition, phasing, and looping, is that the rhythm of the single tone defines the overall structure. The mutation of the single tone creates a perception of change.

Obviously, what I am delving into in my paintings is the line as the "central character" in my work, mutating rhythmically, evolving, forming, and finally even defining the boundaries of the work. In my process, as in allowing the rhythm to take over, I allowed the strokes of my hand – reverberating, traversing – through the visual field to create. This way, my body is language, which was an important issue for me as the line is a direct extension of me creating, the quality of gesture, tension, and intensity of the line influencing the feeling of the specific pieces. The feelings range from anger to violence to sexuality and eventually tranquility. Anger and sexuality are synonymous for me.

Aggressiveness, violence, sexuality, rage, and forging in balance create tranquility, in my opinion. As with my work, I believe the different forces depart and arrive simultaneously, creating a feeling of harmony.

Looking back now at my influences, I realize that the beauty I was able to find in NYC's rough streets, in the creativity of my contemporaries, and in everyday details can all be found in my various works. My journeys among cultures and social contexts, as a child from Iraq to Israel and, later, as an adult from Israel to NYC, have influenced my life experience and inspired my art: being uprooted, experiencing alienation, and eventually settling in. Separation from the familiar, both the family dearest to me and the past I strived to escape. My years of deep study, the strangers I encountered, some becoming my closest friends or strongest influences, the confrontations, and, eventually, the sweet adaptation.

# Arriving

My first arrival to the USA was on October 13th, 1969, at JFK airport. It was bittersweet. It was my first experience of such a large structure. The airport I had departed from in Tel Aviv could not compare. Hordes of people buzzed around from one corner of the airport to the other. It was unnerving to see people so much larger than I was in build. So much taller too! I had not encountered many Africans until this time, and to see so many African Americans taking charge and telling people where to go and what to do was unexpected. Voices were much louder than anything I was accustomed to, as everyone was seemingly yelling at everyone else. It felt to me as if they were yelling at me, too. I did not speak English and these aggressive voices seemed directed at me. My instinct to self-preserve kicked in, and I became more fearful, hoping to avert conflict by not making a single sound in return. I tried my hardest to blend in with the crowd.

What I knew of New York City was from the handful of American movies I had watched in theaters. That was my frame of reference. After the first shock wore off, I began to feel a sense of familiarity with this city that I did not know. Sam, a contemporary of mine who I knew from Tel Aviv, Israel, came to New York one year prior and was meeting me at the airport.

Sam was pale, blonde, and overweight. He blended into the crowd and was comfortable engaging with our surroundings. He spoke the language, and I soon started to sense a patronizing tone in how he spoke to me. It felt to me like I embarrassed him by not speaking the English language. Sam had, by this point, found a job in New York City, which was my highest priority. He was, in hindsight, the person who gave me the nudge I needed to take the risk and come to New York. He encouraged me over our short and frequent phone calls and sent postcards inviting me to join him in New York. It took me a year of coaxing to gather the courage to make that journey across the Atlantic to a world I knew so little about.

Within hours of arrival, it became clear to me that settling in would not be as natural for me as it was for him. Sam, in his first year, had made the adjustment to assimilate into the culture of New York City, the melting pot that embraced with open arms people from different cultures and diverse backgrounds. Sam had insisted on renting a car to pick me up from the airport and, after the fact, asked me to pay the fee. I arrived in the US with my life savings of $500. I was understandably very anxious about my limited resources and how long it would take me to find a stable source of income.

What awaited me at his shabby fifth-floor walk-up apartment on the Upper West Side of Manhattan at 83$^{rd}$ and Broadway was not a pretty sight. The roof was leaking, and I had never seen anything so dirty or so many cockroaches running for cover when the lights were turned on. It was not until we dropped off my luggage at his apartment that Sam clarified that he wanted me to contribute $80 a month for my share of the rent as his roommate. I was extremely exhausted from the flight and the jetlag. That being said, all I could think of was how much money was left in my pocket, having spent $120 of my savings within hours of arriving. I was beginning to develop a fear that my money would run out faster than I could replenish it. I went to bed with the numbers rolling in my head, wondering what the new day would bring. The next morning, after breakfast, Sam instructed me to open a bank account and deposit $300 so we could take advantage of the current offering – a free set of coffee mugs as a welcome gift for new customers. I did not recognize this as the good advice it was, opening a bank account. I just felt obliged to do it so I could avoid conflict with my friend and the only person I knew here. I did not know the "rules" of friendship in our new environment, and I was doing what I thought was right in order to accommodate my friendship with Sam. In my first

# Tribe of One

24 hours in the new city, I was left with only $80 in my pocket.

I needed to start working immediately and, at the same time, look for an art school that would enable me to stay in the country (on a legal visa) and to keep pursuing my art education. These were the reasons I came to the United States. I had not completed my art education in Israel and I wanted to master my knowledge with a new direction in the art world. My languages, limited as they were, were Arabic and Hebrew. I barely spoke English, and I expected that finding work and study would be exceptionally challenging. Searching for a job where I could use my native language led me to an opening at the Israeli Consulate at minimum wage. I found myself in the basement at the Consulate, xeroxing and printing flyers to be handed out to groups supporting Israel, as well as other mundane office work.

I hated that job, but I knew I could not give it up without landing something more appealing. It became abundantly clear to me that my limited English language skills were a handicap that I needed to overcome. Fortunately, I was accepted to the Brooklyn Art School despite this. It was an afternoon graduate program, and I would start my day at 7 am at the Consulate, then hurry down to Brooklyn for class. The subway was a jarring experience and a reliable way to get to school by 4 pm. My teacher and mentor at school was the great Japanese sculptor Toshia Odate. His English was as lousy as mine, and this was one of the many reasons he seemed to develop empathy towards me. We bonded, comparing cultures and describing our respective homes, sharing a drink after class from time to time, and talking about art and our new lives in New York. Late in the evening, after school, I would ride the subway back to SoHo, where, at a loft on Prince Street and West Broadway, I was apprenticing with an Israeli sculptor, Yehuda Ben-Yehuda. While this was unpaid work, it influenced me very much and connected me to the downtown art community.

I usually would be home on the Upper West Side by midnight, then steal a few hours of sleep and wake up to repeat this routine day after day.

# Allen Street

The Lower East Side, generally, and Allen Street, specifically, were notoriously shady. In the early 20$^{th}$ century, it was littered with brothels and had become a home to vagrants, the homeless, drug dealers, and hot goods peddlers. It was also a neighborhood where penniless artists could afford to live in inexpensive large studios. The stench of human urine on the streets was unbearable. The homeless were everywhere, and needless to say, there was no place for them to shower and get clean, so there was a sour odor attached to them that one could smell from blocks away.

At the end of the night, the cheap restaurants would toss the leftover food on the streets for stray cats and dogs, though they, too, seemed to reject this. The artists living in the neighborhood would inevitably find ways to communicate with these downtrodden individuals, probably because we shared with them the rejection of the mainstream society that saw us as unproductive members, aimlessly going about our days instead of working. This is where I met the sculptor Yehuda Ben-Yehuda, near his studio in that area.

Yehuda, himself, had a huge head of black curly hair, which I don't think he ever washed. It had its own unique scent and I must admit, I grew to like it. Most of the time, he walked barefoot, wearing wide, loose-fitting trousers. In a strange way, the trousers always seemed pristine and clean, much more so than his actual skin or hair. I regularly wondered if he ever took a shower. Leaving Ben Yehuda's studio loft late at night, I would be weary of encountering one of those unsavory characters. At that time, I did not understand or realize that, in large part, those people were not hostile or aggressive and that they mostly minded their own business. I eventually learned that their primary concerns were when and where they would have their next bottle of wine or drug fix. If there was any communication between them and others, it was only to ask for some change to pay for that next fix.

During the day, Allen Street was very much alive and buzzing with a diverse mix of people, some residing in the nearby low-income housing and others merchants, mainly in the clothing (Shmata) business, selling their wares cheaper than merchants in other parts of town. As the night got darker, the respectable merchants abandoned Allen Street, and the downtrodden took over. The streets were buzzing once again with drugs, prostitution, and the drunk. The new cycle of life began again.

At Yehuda's studio, I learned a great deal about sculpture – specifically, I learned about latex. Yehuda's work at the time focused on casting human bodies in plaster. That cast plaster became the negative of a human body, which we would then cast latex rubber inside. It is the same process as casting in bronze or any other material. You must cast first the shell, and the shell becomes the negative and within it the body which is the positive itself.

Like many of his generation at that time, Yehuda was a conceptual sculptor. He was casting the plaster from live models and turning them into latex-rubber full-size versions of a human being. The nature of the material, flexible and jelly-like, in Yehuda's work allowed him to create his concept, piling one body on top of another. These piles of bodies were reminiscent of soldiers at war or Jews during the Holocaust. He would connect these latex bodies to an electric source, creating vibrations through a generator, giving the impression of a body under great distress.

Most of what I know about plaster, rubber, and latex was from the work I did with Yehuda Ben-Yehuda.

# Susan the Welsh

A year into my new life in the United States, I met Matania, an Israeli-born pilot who flew for Southwest Airlines. He was fascinated by the art world and saw it as a glamorous and romantic place. He enjoyed rubbing shoulders with people involved in the art world. He felt that he could become part of that world by simply hanging out with those involved in the arts.

Matania was a guitarist. Although I never heard him play, I heard that he was a talented musician. From what I could tell, he was a frustrated musician who never had the opportunity to make a living pursuing his music, and instead, he defaulted to working as a pilot. He fantasized about the glamour of the art world that he aspired to be a part of. He found that hanging with artists provided some degree of vicarious pleasure, belonging, and young, beautiful women. During that period, it was considered romantic to belong to the art world and socialize with young, attractive women.

To Matania's credit, he tried to help artists by representing them and selling their work. That gave him the feeling of belonging. In doing so, he invited me to his home in suburban Richfield, Connecticut. He wanted to show me that he already had some other artists, mainly sculptors, who were in his group that he "represented." He showed me the different pieces in his possession. To add to the excitement, he mentioned that he was married to a young Welch woman named Susan, whom he described as very athletic and beautiful. He, himself, was a big guy and a charmer. He used to visit New York City from his mansion in Connecticut to hang out with artists. We would go for drinks, and he would attempt to impress me with his lifestyle and desire to be an art dealer.

I was eager to find somebody to listen to me and hoped that he would be able to assist me as an art dealer, as he aspired to be. The combination of an artist and an art dealer is a peculiar relationship, with each one working to leverage the other's talents and enhance their success. The reality was and is that in this relationship, each tries to get something from the other. Our relationship continued to develop, and he eventually invited me to spend the weekend at his home with his family: his young Welch wife and his three-year-old daughter. He made it sound very exciting, explaining that his wife was like me, an avid tennis player. Tennis was one of the few sports I picked up growing up in Israel, albeit not with proper training, but I could still swing and hit the ball to where it needed to land. I accepted his invitation with lots of enthusiasm and a little bit of trepidation since weekend visits to the countryside were not part of my lifestyle. He and his family welcomed me upon arrival, and I was taken with his wife, Susan, a strong woman with pale Welch skin, flaming red hair, and mesmerizing green eyes. Coming from the Middle East, I had a fascination with blondes or red-haired women. She was even more attractive to me when she began to speak with her crisp English accent. I enjoyed listening to her talking even though I did not understand half of what she was saying.

Susan had managed to assimilate into the American suburban lifestyle and seemed to enjoy it very much. In those days, living in a big house was a sign of achievement. It was clear that this was different from the place of her origin. Susan's father was a judge in her native England, and she grew up in a very conservative household. Moving to America was equivalent to changing her way of life and going towards a more open society, particularly during that era. Shortly after meeting Susan, I was introduced to their toddler daughter having just woken up from her afternoon nap.

I sat there watching Matania, Susan, and their daughter, Tamar, staring back at me in awkward silence. None of us knew how to start the conversation, as we seemingly had so little in common. That was my first time visiting anyone for an extended weekend stay. I was not sure what my hosts expected while spending a weekend or how to respond when they took me on the house tour, showing their home from one room to the other. They were so proud of what they achieved and accumulated. I did not know how to respond to what they were showing me… the furniture, the grounds, and all that goes with a suburban home. I developed an immediate fear of not responding appropriately and simply wanted to be left alone. I could guess that as a guest, it was incumbent upon me to participate and appropriately compliment my hosts. That was my first introduction to what an American lifestyle looked like.

Susan and I went to play tennis as her husband had suggested earlier; she was a very good player. We enjoyed each other's company. It was easy to talk to her, and she didn't seem to mind my broken English. I learned that she had spent a year living in Israel and spoke some Hebrew. She seemed very proud to converse with me. The weekend was a bit strange, and I left unsure if I had met my hosts' expectations, highlights being my playing tennis with Matania's attractive wife and his showing me his collection of sculptures. I had no interest in the type of work he collected. He was very proud of his collection and tried to find a market for his Israeli-made sculptures that he had brought back to New York. By the end of the weekend, I was exhausted and very happy to return to my shabby apartment in New York City. I did develop an interest in his red-haired wife and hoped in my heart to see her again.

# Tribe of One

A few weeks after my visit, I received a call from Susan. She was going to be in the city and invited me to meet her at a café. I happily agreed, and I felt that my secret wish to see her again had been granted. The day of our meeting went very nicely, and I was thrilled that she made the first move since she was my friend's wife, and I did not dare ask to see her again. Sometime after this meeting, she called me again and asked if I would like to have lunch with her. That was fun, too, and after lunch, we went to see a movie. I learned that once a week, Susan would come into the City for the day, as was common for suburban housewives to do. We sat at the movie theater in complete darkness and silence, except for the sound from the movie screen. I felt the desire and dared to touch her arm, and she responded to me by leaning over, and we started kissing. At the end of the movie, Susan went back home to Connecticut, and this weekly rendezvous became our weekly ritual.

During this time, I lived on 89$^{th}$ Street and 1$^{st}$ Avenue in a railroad apartment. It was my first experience living in this type of apartment, with a long corridor and rooms on one side of the corridor. I shared this apartment with two other flatmates. We were busy working side jobs, so the apartment remained empty for most of the day. When Susan came to visit me in that apartment, she was fascinated by my lifestyle and its stark contrast to hers in Connecticut. I moved to this apartment after my relationship with my flatmate Sam turned sour, and we could no longer enjoy one another's company. From my perspective, he began to behave like a rooster in a hen house. I did not have much communication with my new flatmates. We were in different worlds, as three foreigners trying to survive life in New York. At that time, that part of the Upper East Side was called Germantown, after the predominant German culture. I enjoyed the German food in our neighborhood since I ate similar food in Israel, where I grew up through my teenage years.

As my relationship with Susan developed, we both realized that we could not continue seeing each other in that apartment with three flatmates, and I began to look for a place where we could find more privacy. Susan's reality changed day by day as she realized that she must leave her husband. She could no longer be with him and keep developing a closer relationship with me. Whenever Matania was out of town for his job, Susan and I would spend the time together. I would take the train to stay with her day in and day out, discovering the sweetness of illicit and constant lovemaking.

Eventually, my absence started taking its toll on my work and commitments back in the city, and it became very difficult for me to continue traveling to Connecticut with such regularity. We both agreed to move our relationship forward and create a stable environment for this. I started to look for a suitable apartment that would accommodate the two of us.

I found an apartment on 17th Street and 8th Avenue, which, at that time, was a cheap option and mostly populated by low-income Spanish-speaking people, as well as gay men and lesbians. That mix of people created a beautiful and harmonious population. Street life had a cheerful vibe. Susan declared to her husband that she was leaving him and her daughter, and she moved in with me.

# Tribe of One

To help support us, Susan found work at an AVIS Rent-A-Car during the day and went to Columbia Law School at night. Matania, who realized that Susan had managed to survive and was not going to return to him in Connecticut, developed extreme jealousy. He would not allow her to see her three-year-old daughter. He harassed us by calling constantly, mostly in the middle of the night. He started a custody battle with Susan, declaring her an unfit mother. The court gave him exclusive custody.

Susan and I lived together like this for a couple of years. We both struggled financially and emotionally; Susan, because she could not see her daughter, working and studying around the clock, and I, also working my hardest at various jobs and still unable to find financial security. Our lives eventually took a turn, and our love started to show the cracks of the everyday struggle to survive the big city. I had not had a long-term relationship with anyone before Susan and was beginning to understand the challenges of this. It was not as easy as I had imagined to communicate and keep the embers of our love burning. Matania continued to call us in the middle of the night and threatened to report me to immigration if I did not leave Susan. My fear of being kicked out of the country haunted me. I was not familiar with immigration law, and I was extremely worried. Could he do that? I had no one to turn to for reliable information and could not afford the legal consultation fees of an immigration lawyer.

What kept Susan and I together was our love and mutual need for one another, but the weight of our troubles was starting to pull us apart.

# The Edge of the Precipice

I was a heavy smoker, and I was beginning to cough regularly and intensely. That was when I was working as an assistant to the sculptor, Ben Yehuda. I spent many hours in his studio, assisting him in casting the latex figures into the desired shapes. I realized that something was terribly wrong. I did not have health insurance, but I learned from friends that I could go to Bellevue Hospital as they admitted patients without health insurance, free of charge.

At Bellevue, the doctors and nurses could not relate to the challenges of people like me – the poor, hungry artists, or general outcasts. Yet, as patients, we were treated with dignity and kindness. We were taken care of equally to others who had insurance. I trusted the doctors who would be taking care of me. After they realized that I was a heavy smoker, they gave me a chest x-ray and discovered a tumor in my lung. I had no prior records of my health, and it was, therefore, impossible to ascertain whether that tumor had been there for a long time. There was no conclusiveness as to whether the tumor was malignant or benign. I don't think I properly understood the significance or implications of this tumor, so I could not appreciate the seriousness of this diagnosis. The doctor, at that time, asked me to find a record of prior x-rays to compare these results to and better determine the seriousness of my condition.

I got in touch with a friend in Israel and pled him to inquire at the military office of records for my health records from the time of my army service. While we waited for this, the doctors scheduled my lung surgery, regardless, to determine whether the tumor was malignant. The evening before going to the hospital for the surgery, Susan and I invited a few friends over to my apartment on 17th Street and shared with them, for the first time, my plans for surgery the following day.

To some degree, I felt brave proceeding with the procedure, not knowing what would be involved and how dangerous it could potentially be. The following morning, Susan joined me at the hospital and took my street clothes back home, with the intention of bringing clean clothes following my procedure. I put on the hospital gown and got in the line of patients awaiting their surgery that day. That was when the gravity of my predicament finally dawned on me. The feeling in the hospital, even if you are not sick, seeing so many sick people around you, you begin to develop a fear of your own mortality.

At the hospital, the nurses hurried past from one room, or patient, to the other. The doctors shouted orders constantly. There was a clear sense of chaos, although they presumably knew what they were doing. Eventually, a group of doctors came to my bed, and the lead doctor explained to a group of interns standing around my bed what my condition entailed. They peppered me with questions, and every question became a heavy burden for me to answer since my English was still limited at this time, having only been in the US for about a year. The doctors seemed confident that as a young and strong patient, the surgery would succeed. After the group left my bedside and moved on to the next patient in the room, I developed a monumental fear of what was about to happen to me. A sudden and intense need to flee dawned on me, and I started to plan my escape from the hospital. It was as if I was in jail.

I had noticed that the hospital had guards, nurses, and other caretakers, and I appreciated that escaping was going to be a big ordeal. I was not left alone very much, and I was watched 24/7 by various caretakers. I made up my mind that I would not go through with the surgery scheduled for the following morning.

The hospital allowed visitors in the late afternoon and early evening, and I decided that this would be the best window to attempt my escape in, as people milled in and out, and foot traffic was heaviest and most distracting to the hospital staff. Susan had taken my personal clothes, so I couldn't even change these hospital clothes. I called a friend, Bill Stuart, an artist-sculptor, and I told him about my dilemma and my desire to leave the hospital. At that time, in order to leave the hospital, somebody had to sign for you or obtain permission from the medical staff that I no longer needed to stay in the hospital. Bill was shocked when I told him my plans, and he begged me to reconsider and to go through with the surgery. I convinced him that I did not want to do the surgery and that I needed his help in this small window within which I could leave. I asked him to go to my studio on the corner of Crosby and Broome Street to fetch some clothes and to bring them to the hospital for me. I was determined to walk out of the hospital surreptitiously without the required doctor's permission.

Bill reluctantly accepted the idea, and he brought my clothes. I changed into them and sat with him in the hospital cafeteria for a short time before we walked out of the hospital, just as visitors do. Back at home on 17th Street, Susan was surprised and shocked, not appreciating or supporting my decision not to proceed with the surgery. Shortly after I left the hospital, the staff realized I was no longer there, and we started to receive endless phone calls to return to the hospital and to continue the course of treatment they had recommended, beginning with the surgery. They doubled their efforts when they realized I was not returning and continued to call for days and days, trying to alert us to the seriousness of my medical condition and the risks I was taking. I promised to return, knowing I was not going to do so, just to get them off my back.

My friend, Ben Yehuda, the sculptor to whom I was an assistant, suggested that I go to a private doctor associated with NYU to do a biopsy only in order to confirm the status of the tumor. I did, and the diagnosis was inconclusive, but the tumor appeared to be benign. They asked me to come in another three months for another biopsy and to continue doing so for that first year and in the years to come.

Today, that tumor is still in my lung after all those years, and as I like to think, has become the guardian of my life.

# Dawn in the Occident

My second major relationship in New York City was with Maria, from the former Yugoslavia. She was, similar to me, an outsider with an easygoing nature, enjoying the company of others, laughing, partying, and dancing – for fun and for a living. She regularly drank alcohol and did recreational drugs. It was not in my nature to keep up with those activities on a daily basis. She worked as a go-go dancer in New York City clubs, as did many young women who came from Eastern Europe.

I had not shared very much with Maria about my background or the time I spent in Israel, yet I invited her to join me on my trip to visit my family. Maria's Slavic background enabled her to connect easily with my family in Israel. There were many similarities in the history of the Ottoman Empire and its descendants, including the food, the music, the dance, the culture, and other traditions. This and her open nature facilitated her connection with my family. They embraced Maria almost immediately, probably because they did not know how she earned her living in New York. Together with Maria, I had the best time on that visit to Israel. Maria, albeit not Jewish, was able to connect to everyone we encountered, and I took the opportunity to visit much of Israel with her, both to show her a good time and to discover many of these towns myself.

This auspicious adventure was overshadowed by our initial arrival in Israel. It was a few months after the Yom Kippur War, also known as the Fourth Arab-Israeli War, that the whole environment in Israel became one of fear and deep concern for the safety of the country. Coming from a Middle Eastern country, my olive skin made me look "suspicious," unlike the many Central and Eastern European citizens of Israel. At the airport, while Maria was being waved through customs, I was pulled out of the line and brought to an interrogation trailer. The ensuing interrogation lasted for several hours before I was finally allowed to enter the country and pick up my bags, where Maria was waiting for me. The airport was colorful in its diversity of people, languages, and cultures. Some people looked suspicious, while others looked like outsiders, all carrying packages in different colors and shapes. You could tell from each person arriving that they were searching for familiar faces or recognition of where they were. It almost resembled a scene from a harmonious market. The interrogators were polite and friendly and, thankfully, eventually realized that I did not pose a threat. They recognized from my accent that we were all Israelis. It was apparent that because Israel had just survived another territorial war and repelled a coalition of Arab states, enemies were suspected everywhere, and terrorist threats were in abundance.

This unfortunate incident – not being welcomed in my own homeland and being treated as a possible enemy of the State of Israel – was a humiliating experience, particularly in front of Maria, who had no background or understanding of the politics and history of Israel and the relationships with neighboring Arabs. Here again, I felt like an outsider in the country of my citizenship and the place I was supposed to call home.

This experience was traumatic and stayed with me for many years; it ultimately overshadowed the many positive moments of my visit. This incident contributed to my ambivalence in seriously considering a return to Israel.

## Accidental Presumptions

I would have been presumptuous to assume that when I first arrived in NYC, I would have been received with open arms. As a matter of fact, I anticipated that everyone would be waiting for me and that they would treat me like an important person. I quickly realized that none of that was going to happen since, in life, nothing happens as one expects. More often than not, things go the other way around, and many things happen completely by accident. Mainly being there, in the right place, at the right time, and perhaps being in the right state of mind, I realized quickly enough that NYC was welcoming, but at the same time, it kept you at arm's length, and the feeling that you were going to be accepted vanished quickly. You began to learn, the hard way, that to be accepted, you had to be one of them and not in competition with them.

And so, I learned that in order to survive and not come across as needy, I had to hold different jobs at the same time. By doing so, I removed the pressure on others to liberate them from the feeling that they needed to help me.

I discovered during the course of my journey that I was like many before me, who had just arrived on the shores of a new country with nothing more than their dreams and hopes that everything would be taken care of. Those dreams vanished as quickly as the weather changed. So, I learned that life abroad, as an outsider, would be hard and that I must accept and compromise with my reality. I was not alone. I went on to meet other artists in similar circumstances who felt the same way. I could communicate with them, based on our experiences, trying to break through the wall of being newcomers. I met those people mainly at school in the Brooklyn Art Museum.

My teacher was a Japanese artist. The head of the school was German, and the student body was equally international and similar in age, having come to NYC to start their respective careers. We all shared the dream that we would be received with open arms and that our careers would flourish just because we ventured from elsewhere with new ideas that had not been used yet. We learned soon enough that new ideas belonged to fantasy and that the culture itself and skills that existed in NYC were hard to break through. Therefore, my peers and I learned that in the established art scene, conceptual and minimalist, where one was able to sell one's art, one was labeled as commercial or exceptional superstar.

The insider artists were American-born and were schooled at Ivy Leagues, such as Yale, Columbia, or RISD. They were considered the top of the top. They created their own groups and had their own galleries; critics supported their thinking, and it was impossible for outsiders to break into that circle.

My ability to express myself in English was very limited. Culturally and socially, I was inept compared to the circle of American artists who guarded themselves and didn't allow outsiders into their groups. In that generation, which, at the time, was called Minimalist Art, there was more talking than doing. That concept was valued at the time, and it was cherished by all foreign artists who were working to enter this circle and to be accepted. Yet, it was purely American art, and not influenced by any other schools (European).

I myself was gravitating to the community of artists who, like me, were outsiders to the NYC scene, such as my teacher and mentor, the Japanese sculptor, Toshio Odate. Toshio himself was an outsider and barely spoke English. He was a conceptual artist, yet no one understood exactly what he was trying to do. Conceptual art, by its definition, required that it be verbally defended to an eloquent and cerebral elite who primarily mastered English. They loved semantics and emerged from the American-based Ivy League art schools.

# Tribe of One

As much as I would have liked to have been fluent in both, for me, there was a separation between the homo faber and the homo lumens category of artists. I could not cross over. I eventually learned that I was clearly in the homo faber category, searching for a way to make an impact with materials and processes. The artists who influenced my work were often of the same category. This led me to create and work with plaster and latex in my early years in NYC (1970-1972).

# At the River of Babylon

When I close my eyes, I still remember the town near Baghdad, where I was born. The scene gets confused with my reality, so much so that it becomes distorted. Besides the culture, nature, the landscape, the air, and the scents were so different from where I am now. At times, it feels like it wasn't me who lived there.

At times, I miss that feeling, but I cannot simplify it. I know the smell was different, but I do not recognize the scent today. The brightness of the light burned my eyes. That does not exist in my new reality, and I cannot compare it to where I am now. The landscape that I was born and reared in cannot be compared to anything around me. At times, I feel that the person born into that little town is not someone I recognize. I could not recognize myself in the places I was born and the environment I grew up in. Besides, the language, which is totally different from the one I use today, kept me apart mentally and emotionally – the sound of the speaking language, the rhythm of the language, the way the lips move and the tone flows… it was all different. In addition to adopting the new culture, I also needed to adapt the speed and sound of my voice. At times, my voice was too high or too low, and people around me would ask me to repeat myself. I tried to adapt myself to my new rhythm of talking, and that confused me, as it required more than I was ready for.

I was born at home, and there was nothing special about that. At that time, and in that culture, women did not give birth in hospitals. Babies were born at home. That brought health complications, and some newborns struggled without the necessary medical attention. I was born into a family of seven children, and I was the second to last. My parents were anxious because they had lost a son born immediately before me. They felt the necessity to have another male child amongst the daughters. There were five daughters, and I was the only son who survived.

I was closely watched and protected by all my sisters and mother. Their efforts were exacerbated by the fear of losing the second son. I was not allowed any privacy nor the chance to play with other children, unchaperoned by at least one of my sisters. That limited my ability to establish my independence and make my own decisions.

I do remember contracting chicken pox at age four. To comfort me, I was sat on a donkey's back, and one of my sisters would lead it on a tour of the town. I must say I enjoyed it very much, and that was my first experience riding the back of an animal. In a strange way, I felt aroused on the ride, sitting high and watching the town go by. It gave me a feeling of superiority to have been singled out amongst my sisters as the special son who got special treatment.

My parents were a product of the early 1900s. My father was born in 1910, and my mother in 1916. Both came from large families with traditional structures. My father came from Northern Iraq, on the border with Iran, for an arranged marriage to my mother, an Iraqi-born teenager with roots from the 19$^{th}$ century. That itself was no surprise since, in those times, most marriages were arranged, and some were even within related families. This was mainly because of financial necessity or tradition. The eligible bachelor played the hunter role, pursuing his mate, starting his family, and establishing his independence. My father was a talented goldsmith who honed his skills from a young age, apprenticing and doing odd and small jobs to earn his living. When he settled with my mother in our little town, he opened his jewelry shop.

My mother, at that time, was a homemaker. She never had a job outside of caring for the home and family. I vaguely remember my father returning home every afternoon for lunch and the siesta that followed. In the hot afternoons, one of us children was responsible for fanning him during his nap so he could be cool and comfortable. At the time, I had mixed feelings about that responsibility. Was this a privilege, or was it punishment? After waking up, my father would reward the fanner with a piece of candy and an appreciative smile. Needless to say, the house sat in complete silence while he napped. Nothing moved or risked disturbing his peace.

I was born in 1941, even though, in official documents, it is listed as 1940. The change happened when we arrived as refugees in Israel in 1949. My father aged each of the members of our family by one year so we would qualify for larger social support payments from the government. My birth name was Zacharia, and at home, they called me Zaki.

As Iraqi Jews, my family lived side by side with our Iraqi Muslim countrymen. The relationships were great between the religions. Jews were widely accepted in the community, living side by side with other religions. As a child, I recall playing with my neighbor, who was Muslim. I did not know the difference, and I don't believe that he did either. As a shy child, I was always invited to play with the neighbors' kids. It was easy for them to play with me because I would have listened to them and not objected to them changing the rules of the games we played. Within the regional culture, we were all semitic, and we had similar color skin; therefore, as children, we all looked alike. I was perhaps smaller and constantly guarded by my sisters, which confused the on-lookers.

During that period, in the early 1940s, things began to change, mainly with Hitler's expansion of the Reich, and the ideas of Nazism began to flourish throughout the Middle East. It was mainly when the Reich soldiers arrived in North Africa, to the Middle East, and then to what was, at the time, the Kingdom of Iraq.

The Iraqi King Faisal, rather than entering the war with Nazi Germany, similar to other tribes and countries in the Middle East, began to sympathize with the Nazi regime and its ideologies. This gave him more influence and power in Iraq and the Middle East. Until that point, the Jewish people lived in Iraq very happily – some of them were advisors and ministers in the king's court, mainly in managing the country's finances. The king at the time trusted his Jewish advisors, and that was the best era of Jewish life in Iraq. They were well-to-do, the intellectual elite. At that time, King Faisal trusted and protected Jewish Iraqis from discrimination.

This changed as the German Reich became powerful in the Middle East as many heads of governments and tribes wanted to avoid potential conflict with the powerful Nazi army. Instead, they began sharing information and distanced themselves from the local Jewish populations, driving the relationship in a very different direction. Secrecy took the place of the previous trust, and the religions became suspicious of one another. Jewish people were afraid to show themselves. We went into hiding lest we be discovered.

At that time, in another part of the world, the Zionist movement had started in a backroom in Eastern European countries like Austria and Poland. The movement started in the 1900s, with one of the major influences and political activists, Theodore Hertzel, the father of Zionism. He formed the Zionist organization in Eastern Europe and ignited the flame and idealistic heart of the Jewish belief. Until that time, the Jewish people in Europe never considered leaving their respective countries, where most of them fared well financially and otherwise. Until then, they had not felt the need or desire to leave that part of the world.

As Nazis became more powerful, beginning in 1932, the Jewish Europeans realized that they must find an exit, just in case they were further harassed. It was in 1939, when the Crystal Nacht occurred, where Jewish businesses and homes were marked with the Jewish star and targeted or looted, that the Jewish community realized for the first time that they were in danger. Until that point, they felt protected by the law, their businesses flourished, and their communities coexisted safely with others.

My father joined the Zionist movement. As the Zionist missionaries arrived in Baghdad from Israel, they would stay in homes like ours and preach the glory of relocating to the Jewish state of Israel. That was the first time I encountered that community, and when they asked me my name and when they realized that it was an Arabic name, Zaki, they instructed my father to change my name to a Jewish Zionist Biblical name. The one they chose for me was Bar-cochva, a heroic Hebrew and Biblical name. All of a sudden, I changed into that new name with a different personality, and I felt as if I was a chosen one, with the responsibility of a new role to play, to legitimize and earn my new name. This happened a few months shy of my sixth birthday. I later realized how much of a burden that name change bore upon me. Needless to say, I quickly, and have since, hated that name.

Around that time, King Faisal took some pages from the Nazi ideology and decided it was time to push the Iraqi Jews out of the country. That came as a surprise and created much chaos in our lives after many years of peace and prosperity in our home country. The tensions between the religions exacerbated the mistrust among us.

As the Jewish people continued to withdraw from society, we also started to transfer our wealth and assets into gold or other valuable goods so they could be easily carried when we were ready to flee. The streets became unsafe, and businesses feared losing overnight the wealth that they had accumulated over the years. It was around 1948 that Palestine became the State of Israel, and the Jewish families started to consider the benefits of relocating to Israel, leaving behind businesses, homes, and friends.

My father decided to escape to Israel, not through legal immigration, a concept not yet established, but rather through smugglers. The nine of us crossed the borders in a lorry truck, with whatever of our assets he could transfer to gold. The women hid the gold in their clothes and covered it with their veils. The route took us from Baghdad through Iran and Syria before we finally arrived in Israel. Our lorry arrived at the Iraqi/Iranian border at sunrise, at which point the smugglers ran away, and we were left at the mercy of the border patrol.

## Tribe of One

As they searched us, they took most of the gold my mother and sisters carried and reported us to the Iraqi authorities, who, in turn, loaded us into a different lorry and carried us back to Baghdad jail, where we remained for three weeks. My older sister was pregnant and ended up going into labor on the drive back to Baghdad jail. The newborn daughter was named Joon, a derivation of the word "sijn," or jail, in Arabic, our mother tongue at the time.

The whole family was locked up together in one jail cell, sleeping on the floor. We were eventually released without any of our possessions or citizenship. My father was forced to sign a document that he had no claim on any assets in Iraq, and in return, the family was put on the next flight to Cyprus. From there, we were flown to Israel two days later.

# At the Refugee Camp

Upon arrival, we were carried to a refugee camp. At this first registration with the Israeli authorities, my name was officially changed to Bar-cochva, and my sisters 'names were similarly changed on the spot to Hebrew names. Najibah became Ora. Senoira became Segura. My mother, Qamar, became Tamar. My father and older brother were the lucky ones; they remained Shlomo and Benjamin, respectively, having been born to Hebrew names.

The refugee camp we were housed in was comprised of tents, one for each family. Metal beds were provided, and the nine of us shared these. I, being so young, would lay with my sisters while each of my parents had a bed of their own. We lived like this for the better part of a year, waiting for what came next. The food we received was delivered by volunteers and primarily consisted of bread, butter, and chocolate donated by the USA. You would think a child would enjoy a diet of bread, butter, and chocolate, but, in fact, I hated it. The large tub of butter sitting in our tent was our only sustenance.

My grandparents on my mother's side stayed in Iraq. They lived in a different part of town and did not join us in attempting to escape. We had no way of communicating with them, and to this day, we know nothing of what became of them – how much longer they lived or what their remaining time was like. There wasn't telephone communication in those days, and mail was unreliable. We didn't have an address in the refugee camp, nor did we have an address for my grandparents.

Three years after our arrival in Israel, we learned of my grandmother's arrival with my uncle. My grandfather had died bearing arms. He was taken to fight with the Iraqi army. We were able to contact my grandmother and uncle while they were stationed in another refugee camp. My grandmother was very old by then, and she managed to earn money by selling sunflower seeds and nuts in the camp. In that harsh reality, there were no schools or teachers. The children, along with the adults, passed the time, waiting for something to happen. Sometimes, there would be someone to play with. We were camped with Jewish refugees from all over the world, speaking different languages – the lack of a common language being a high barrier to creating friendships and community. The Hebrew language was not one any of us refugees spoke.

For my father and older siblings, especially my brother, there were no jobs of any kind. We were just killing time in the camp without a way to earn a living or a language to communicate in. The Austrian, German, Hungarian, and Romanian Jews spoke Yiddish, a respected language at that time. Arabic was not granted the same position and was considered inferior. If you spoke Arabic, you were considered an outsider, speaking the language of the enemy and not the East European elite. This alienated us, the Jews, from the Middle East and North Africa and left us unappreciated and treated with suspicion. Not being able to speak Hebrew, we were shut out of the new promised land.

Communication was limited to our small, closed family. Each culture had its own tradition, and each "tribe" kept to themselves, in no way socializing or fraternizing with one another. Everyone at the camp waited for something to happen; none of us knew what might come next. We learned, in due course, that our survival was dependent on the charity of others – formal donations from non-governmental organizations, primarily the United Nations, or handouts. As it happened, my father's brother had come to Israel 20 years earlier when it was still Palestine. He lived in Jerusalem and, upon hearing of our arrival, came to visit us. Finally, after a year and a half of our residence in the camp, he invited us to join his family. They lived in a small village on the outskirts of Jerusalem that previously belonged to the Palestinians, but in 1948, the state of Israel took it over and moved Jewish settlers into the houses that remained un-destroyed.

In that village, in the middle of nowhere, there was no power or running water and, of course, no telephones. The Israeli government gave us a small prefabricated house surrounded by three acres of undeveloped land. We were also granted a cow, a goat, and a dozen hens. My goldsmith father had to learn how to farm his land to provide for his family. There was not a single support system except for my uncle, who had, many years earlier, moved to this village and became a farmer himself. Once a week, the Israeli authorities would send someone to visit us and guide us on how to farm the land and work the animals. We also received a weekly ration of bread – a dozen loaves to last us the week. We hadn't yet learned how to bake our own, and this rationing was what kept us from starving.

This was around 1950, and I was, by then, about ten years old. My sisters, all older than me except for one, were teenagers. They, along with my brother, farmed the land and cared for the animals. My sole responsibility was to watch them work, as I was once again without access to school or any form of education. We rose before sunrise, at 3 am, to move the irrigation system, a heavy pipe structure, from one location to the next. As we continued our life in no man's land, we lost our identity and traditions, focused our efforts on mere survival, and, therefore, had no energy or desire to practice any religion. We had all changed our first names, and that bore a burden. I learned from my uncle later that our family name, Doktori, was in reference to a great-grandfather who was a well-respected eye doctor.

That reality was most stressful for my father. It was difficult for him to bear the loss of so much while he could not support the family. He fell into a deep depression soon after our arrival to the Israeli camps. This worsened in our new home in the village, where he could not maintain control over his family.

In our culture, as the father, he was the head of the family, the primary provider, and the decision maker, and he now failed to do either. He couldn't speak the language or be productive, which made it impossible for him to care for his family. There was not a patriarchal substitute for my father, as my brother was still too young himself. My sisters shared with my brother the burden of putting food on the table. As time went on, my father became asthmatic, and his body deteriorated along with his mental health. His reliance on his children was too hard a blow. He could not accept his role in our new environment and under our circumstances. His health continued to worsen until he was ultimately admitted to the hospital for a day and released to die at home a few days later.

My father's passing came as a shock to us all. It happened very quickly, while he was at the young age of 51. My older brother, as is customary in that culture, now became the head of the family. He himself was still young, ill-prepared to bear the burden of supporting a large family with so little means. My mother had managed to smuggle some of her gold jewelry despite everything that was taken from us through this ordeal. She approached other Arabic-speaking families in the village and succeeded in selling some of this jewelry. With that money, she bought a plot of land closer to Tel Aviv and built a small two-family house. We all shared one, and the second my sister, her husband, and baby Joon lived in. We built the houses ourselves. I was too young to contribute; instead, it was my brother and brother-in-law, with the support of my sisters. Anyone who could work or contribute did.

It was a modest house, but with all the necessities to live comfortably. My brother and I occupied a room, and the second room was for my four sisters and mother. By 1950/51, the legal immigration from Iraq to Israel began to flow, as most Iraqi Jews, approximately 400,000, left the country. Many relocated to England, as Iraq had been a British colony, and others went to Canada. Some of the most affluent families moved to India or China, establishing businesses in their adopted homes. The remainder followed us to Israel, though legally this time, following a formal order to exit Iraq. By then, Israel and Iraq had declared war on one another.

The majority of the Jews didn't leave Iraq voluntarily; it was the home where we accumulated our wealth. The missionaries who benefited from accelerating the Jewish migration to Israel bombed a synagogue in Baghdad, killing 17 Jews. This heightened the fears of the Jewish Iraqis and worked as intended to hasten their relocation to Israel.

# The Final Farewell

I was 11 years old when my father died. As I was the youngest son and second youngest in the household, my older brother became the man of the house. It was tradition to say goodbye to a passing family member by visiting the corpse before burial as it lay covered with white sheets on a marble counter. This was to prepare the corpse to be washed. The tradition dictated that this would be the last time the family saw the person they loved. It was a very traumatic experience for me, seeing my father motionless and knowing that he was no longer with us. We had just been together a few days prior; every muscle on his face was responding to our conversations. Now, here he was, with the palest skin, the blood having stopped flowing in his veins. His face was expressionless, with closed eyes. Standing in front of my father's corpse, I was taken aback. Startled by what I saw, I couldn't comprehend what was expected of me at that moment. *Should I allow my tears to flow? Or just hold my sadness in my heart as I was being watched by the people working on washing my father?* It was a tremendous pressure, knowing I was being watched by everyone else in the room as they tried to read my emotions at that moment. It was very difficult for me to respond to my father's corpse lying in front of me, with the added pressure of that environment.

After the corpse washing was completed, my brother and I joined the rest of the family in the small funeral, where my father was buried in the earth and left to rest for eternity. As I was not religious at the time, my mother compelled me to pray and read the Hebrew "Kadish" on my father's soul. To appease her, I repeated this multiple times in an attempt to honor my father.

My mother was still young herself, barely 40 years old. She reacted emotionally over losing my father and cried incessantly. Sometimes, I wonder if her tears were truly flowing or were merely a demonstration of loyalty to her husband. It was another week before we went back to our daily routines. I hated seeing my mother crying, even more so as my sisters joined my mother in grieving our loss. All this occurred around the time that I, as a Jewish boy, had a bar mitzvah, celebrating my coming of age into a responsible man. I was angry at the time, holding those around me responsible for the loss of my father. I resented the bar mitzvah and refused the celebration as a declaration of how pained I was.

It was around then that my older siblings began to leave the house to embark on their own independent lives. My sisters, those still unmarried, took jobs outside the home, as did my brother, now that we were closer to Tel Aviv. This was the only way the family could support itself, and everyone pitched in to carry the burden, contributing how they were able to. My mother could not find employment, primarily hindered by her inability to master the language. She continued to be the primary homemaker, staying home to prepare food and care for baby Joon while my sister worked.

My sisters worked in a tobacco factory, rising early in the morning and working well into the evening. We didn't have a mode of transportation at the time, so they walked to the tobacco factory and back, several miles each way. By the time they returned, they were exhausted and stunk of tobacco. It wasn't different for my brother, who worked at a cardboard company. His work was hard and physical. He was in his early 20s by now and had the strength the job demanded.

I started high school, traveling six miles each way to the school, or "ort." My journey started with a long walk to the main road, where I would take a one-hour bus ride each way. I would arrive at school exhausted by my journey, and I hated the time I had to spend there. For me, these were unhappy times as my language skills were lagging behind my peers who had been in Israel longer than I had. This didn't help me make friends in school, so I struggled to communicate with my peers. The other students didn't speak much Hebrew either. The kids were placed in respective grades based on their age, not their educational level. This meant standards were held low – our schooling comprised some history, maths, and crafts so that we could grow into decent citizens later in life. As we didn't speak Hebrew, none of us could quite succeed in performing at a high level. While I recognized the importance of attending school, I really did not want to be there.

At home, we still spoke Arabic but had started to mix some Hebrew words into everyday conversations. Because my mother never learned Hebrew, Arabic remained our primary language at home. I myself was beginning to forget the Arabic language and felt ashamed to speak it since my strongest desire was simply to assimilate with my peers and fit into my new country. My mother and I barely spoke to one another. I insisted on speaking Hebrew, and I had no appreciation of why she couldn't learn our new language. At times, I felt ashamed that my mother never became like my friend's mothers, an Israeli who spoke Hebrew and could fit in. I also resented my siblings. They worked very hard and did not have time to give me the love and attention I so craved and needed. At that point, they were all of marrying age, ready to start their own families. At the time, matchmakers were the popular means of identifying a mate. They would not even come prepared with photographs, just descriptions of the potential suitor. I vividly recall the whispers and arguments when one of my sisters would not like a suitor. My siblings craved partners who came from our own background, Iraqi Jews, to whom they could relate more easily. My sisters eventually went on to marry, although not always someone who fit these demands, only so they could move on in their lives. They moved out of the shared room with our mother and sisters into their own personal spaces. Needless to say, several of them ended up divorced, but that happens much later in our story.

My brother was still sharing a room with me. I would hear him cry, pained by his love for a girl who worked with him, but our family resented her because she was not deemed worthy of my brother. He spared no effort in convincing my mother and uncle that this girl was the right person for him. It got to the point where, to compel my brother to forget the girl, my mother resorted to witchcraft, returning home with some holy water that my brother was tasked with convincing his love interest to drink so he may stop loving her. This situation continued for many months, and my brother eventually gave up so he would not upset the family. In those days, the parents held the final decision-making power, and the children respected that hierarchy, no matter their age or position. He was eventually introduced by the family to a young teenager, a distant cousin – a shy girl who also came from Iraq with little more than her youth to offer. My brother accepted the marriage, but he never fell in love with her. He left our house to start his new life with his young wife. For reasons I do not know, the elders in my family, including my mother, were extremely pleased with the union. They trusted and valued her, having come from our own tribe.

# Tribe of One

My high school graduation was an unhappy event, as most of my grades were failing. My biggest accomplishments were in the athletic classes. My inability to learn the language had hindered my ability to master any of the academic subjects, and this continued to be a handicap for the remainder of my life.

The other challenge for me was that I did not have friends during that time in my life. My poor communication skills, the lack of language, and the large distance between my home and school made it impossible for me to visit them. It was a six-mile separation, with limited transportation. Once I came home, I kept to myself. I could not maintain friendships with children my age. I did not have a social life at this point.

I was also challenged by the fact that I was not proud of my home or background. My mother could not communicate with friends, had I made any. She barely could communicate with me, as it was. She was a heavy-set woman, unable to speak the local Hebrew language, and didn't dress in a modern way. She listened to Arabic music at home, which exacerbated my feelings of shame for her failure to adapt to our new culture. At that time, I held this against her. This discouraged me from inviting friends to my home. As my older siblings continued to grow and expand their lives outside our home, they had their own struggles to adapt culturally, survive financially, and find acceptance in their new home, having not been educated.

My mother and I had grown to a place where our mode of communication was limited to sign language and a few Arabic words. My Arabic language was fading, and I was not interested in restoring it. My vocabulary, when engaging with my mother, continued to deteriorate. We stopped communicating, just exchanging glances and vibrations to guess one another's feelings or needs. Now that I think about it, I feel guilty for not having made more of an effort to accommodate her as my siblings left the house, one after the other, leaving me alone with my mother and younger sister. The three of us lived together and rarely spoke with one another. My sister and I managed to communicate in Hebrew with the world outside our home, leaving my uneducated mother to her lonesome.

My mother never had a formal education to learn reading or writing outside of a few words that she learned alone. When we arrived in Israel, this made it even harder for her to learn the new language and alienated her further. She became more shy and quiet over time. She sympathized with my sister and me, never complaining to us or imposing her wishes on us. She sank into a deep sadness, first for losing her home, followed by her husband, and now the loss of engaging with her children. She stayed home, creating joy for herself, cooking for us, and watching us consume it with zeal. I eventually realized that I did not like her cooking, and in hindsight, I admit she really was not a good cook. As we ate, she sat in front of us, watching us. When I was done eating, she would finish what was left on my plate, which became our ritual – that I leave food on my plate, and she finishes.

# Becoming a Soldier

Around 1958, on my 17th birthday, I began my army service, customarily two and a half years. I was assigned to a Morse code unit, which we used to communicate between army units and the central control unit to or from the battlefield. I hadn't yet become fluent in Hebrew despite having been in Israel for almost ten years. The technical school I graduated from presented me with a diploma qualifying me as a carpenter. Naturally, that field didn't require verbal skills.

I continued to be shy amongst the other soldiers, many having been born in Israel or had arrived from Europe. They were of a larger build and came prepared with more sophisticated skills, therefore ahead of me in many ways, despite their not speaking Hebrew either. I felt like I had been left behind – that I could not, with my small body, compete with them physically or culturally. The European Jews typically spoke several languages, including Yiddish, German, or Hungarian. They were Israel's elite, and they controlled who did what and when. It was a painful time for me. I was smaller physically, shy, and unable to express my thoughts or emotions. I had no confidence and was too intimidated to speak to girls my age. I feared I would be mocked and looked down upon for having been of Iraqi descent. At this stage, I had not started drinking and didn't have much money to spend or attempt to impress one of the girls to go out with me. This heightened my sense of loneliness, even now when I was serving in the army to protect the state of Israel. Female soldiers at that time looked for more heroic men – larger in size and more intellectually savvy. I wasn't one of those superior men, so I didn't attempt to flirt with any of my female peers at that time.

To be the outsider stays with me today. I learned to live with this reality, and, at times, I even attempted to use it to my benefit later on in life. Here I was, feeling my role as the outsider, growing into it, familiarizing myself with it. I was learning to understand and leverage it. It was in the army when I started to do this. I became observant of things, absorbing the details in my environment and the personalities surrounding me. I trained myself to become more sensitive, to communicate without words, and to follow my intuition.

# The Case of Accidental Reality

To describe my life in Israel, we must understand the idea of ACCIDENTAL REALITY and its intrinsic value. My entire life until then, including my early childhood years in Iraq, had been a sequence of accidental, chance occurrences that brought me to Israel and, ultimately, to the life I built for myself there. The concept of FATE is deeply ingrained in Middle Eastern Culture. As a Bavlim, a Babylonian, or a Jew of Iraqi origin, I had been raised in close proximity to other Middle Eastern and Semitic tribes, and I, too, by culture, held similar beliefs engrained in me, whether directly or through cultural osmosis. The concept of accidental reality can be driven by beliefs that are religious, utterly nonreligious, or a combination of both. Some rely on GOD to invoke and navigate FATE; others depend on the concept of the universe to make sense of whatever hand they have been dealt. The rest embrace the absurdity of life and the (gentle) "indifference of the world," as the French Novelist and Philosopher Albert Camus so openly and eloquently described in his novels. My concept of fate was formed by the experience that nothing in my life had been self-chosen until then and that my reality had entirely relied on circumstantial occurrences that led me to this point in my life. This observational deduction, on my part alone, was already different from that of my siblings and family members when it came to the concept of reality. None of my other siblings had a self-observing, self-reflecting, and self-doubting distance from themselves. Neither that nor any other particular sensibility for the world around them, as far as I could tell. My future life should be different for that reason, as this reality that no one, except for my mother, perhaps, understood. Except we were not able to communicate with words. This set me apart – the personal observation and sense of inherent inner truth. This early realization went on to define me, combined with the hours and days I spent with my mother in a nearly non-verbal environment that almost entirely relied on sensing one another and interpreting each other's intense emotions. I reciprocated my mother's (nearly) boundless love toward me dutifully, despite my shame and resentment of her.

I knew that culturally, it was my duty to take care of my mother and to fulfill her needs, which was impossible without a common language. We shared an emotionally incestuous relationship, a co-dependency that allowed no one else in and made me a prisoner at home with a roommate who was my mother.

Once my youngest sister married, all my siblings left the small house we had built and inhabited for years from the little farmhouse dwelling the government had settled us in following the immigration camp. Looking back, these were, no doubt, the formative years of my life and understandably had the biggest impact on my character for the years to come.

As no confidence was originally instilled in me due to the accidental reality I found myself in, namely that of very little encouragement and almost no experience of success, my strongly underdeveloped social skills in a foreign land drove me to be an emotionally shy person, mainly careful and cautious. However – likely due to the many hours I had spent with my mother – I had already expanded my nonverbal communication skills by then. I continued to evolve into a person who relied on nonverbal communication skills, with a wide range of other abilities such as a strong sense of my surroundings, a widened, intuitive awareness, and an almost animal-like instinct for anything or anybody I came directly or indirectly in contact with.

Many years later, upon arriving in New York, it was this very set of skills that would serve and empower me. New York, I came to learn in due course, was a place where anybody could find a new home. That required a certain versatility and resourcefulness, of course, mixed with the appropriate portion of caution and careful observation. Upon arrival in New York, I discovered that it did not matter that I did not speak a word of English nor had a high school diploma or a college degree.

In New York, I found empathy and kindness from strangers that I had not encountered in Israel. I came from a distant place with no expectations of the culture awaiting me. It seemed that everybody wanted to reach out to me with the intention to help. I experienced in this foreign country, many thousand miles from my birthplace, a kindness and acceptance that I had not encountered in my long years in Israel. I came to America with nothing and was, in turn, offered a clean slate – another case of accidental reality.

# The Mystery of the Promised Land

After serving the compulsory 30 months of military service in the Israeli Army, I went back to my mother's home. Her existence in the small house continued just as when the family first moved into it, except now, she was only sharing it with my youngest sister, who had not yet married and moved out. That changed soon after my return when my sister was matched with a suitor, and I remained alone with my mother. I landed a job as a carpenter and furniture designer in the same school I had graduated from before going to military service. This was how I started to support our household, comprised of just my mother and me. What I had already practiced while being in the army, an awareness and sensibility toward the things around me, a nonverbal facility, continued and intensified with my return to living with my mother. Needless to say, I was the only person she interacted with on a daily basis, in addition to our next-door neighbors – my sister and her now-expanded family. Despite my departure and return, I was just an older version of the small, bitter boy I had once been. I didn't take advantage of my physical proximity to my sister's family and made little effort to develop that relationship.

My years away had not changed the fact that I had a very limited rudimentary vocabulary of Arabic, and my mother was still unable to speak any other language. We communicated on a nonverbal, intuitive level, reading each other's subtle gestures and nearly undetectable expressions, only noticeable or significant to one other. This was surely a bizarre and exclusive relationship to onlookers, so I never brought anyone home. Hidden from prying eyes, our secret relationship continued for several years. I taught carpentry and interior design to adults by day, and in the evenings, I pursued my own continued education at an art school, Avni, in Tel Aviv. I first obtained a teacher's Diploma in Carpentry and Interior Design, and at age 22, I started teaching other adults who, after having served in the army, needed to find a vocation and employment. I specialized in Wood Design.

At that time, I was approached by the Israeli Cultural Attache who was on the lookout for promising talents who could contribute in so many needed ways to the new country's culture. Upon his suggestion, and with government funding, I succeeded in writing a book in Hebrew, a manual instruction book on woodwork titled "From the Cabinet to the Chair." I had come full circle and was now a teacher at the Interior Design School ORT, and the teachers who had taught me now became my peers. My Hebrew had improved sufficiently to allow me to now lecture in these technical crafts. I earned what then was considered good money, and based on these most recent successes, I could have lived a carefree existence had it not been for my mother. I bore the weight of our situation at home, the physical and emotional co-dependency.

My mother cooked and waited all hours of the day and night for me to return home for the next meal. Our evenings were spent alone, sharing a meal, listening to Arabic music on our small radio, and conversing with our facial expressions and body language – a reality I shared with no one else, not even with my siblings who married as soon as it was practical. Our loss of my father so early on in our lives required that I become the surrogate for everything my mother had lost: her country, her husband, and her relevance. Instead of having a fuller existence, waiting for my father to come home and engage with him, she focused her time and attention on me. My siblings would never experience the intimacy and implications of this relationship. My mother's love and attachment to me grew in proportion to her isolation, and even though we didn't and couldn't speak about it, I felt the growing intensity of her feelings and of our relationship. When I returned home after a long day, she would serve me dinner and then wait and watch, and when I was finished, she would take my plate and eat my leftovers, even though there was enough food for the both of us. The significance of this ritual remained with me throughout my life. I became conditioned to leave food on my plate, regardless of whether I enjoyed it or if I was still hungry and could have eaten more. My mother's daily waiting for what would be left of my dinner is deeply ingrained in my behavior. I vividly recall watching her consume my leftovers, an act of thinly veiled, indirect physical lovemaking – a sensual ritual that had become a substitute for a physicality she could have only shared with my father.

Today, other than more recently discovering or, rather, unearthing my love for listening to Arabic music of that period, I am still the keeper of our nightly ritual. I do this by not leaving an empty plate nor being the last one to finish a meal while in the company of others.

# The Perils of a New Home

My trials and travails in Israel were not unique to me alone. Israel was not the Promised Land for all Jewish people. From our early days in the Israeli refugee camps and ever more clearly during my service in the Army, I had found that the opportunities and challenges presented to me were different from those presented to many of my peers. Being of Middle Eastern Jewish origin was a disadvantage as the mainly Eastern European, Ashkenazi Jews had set the cultural tone many years before Middle Eastern families like my own came to Israel when the country still was Palestine.

Many Jews who came from Europe before or during the founding of the State of Israel were intellectuals. They were disproportionately highly educated, spoke many languages, and had social skills akin to the European countries they had come from. They were idealistic, scholarly, intellectually passionate, and ingenious; none of the traits that would come directly to mind when thinking of the Iraqi or other Middle Eastern Jews. The culture of the Ashkenazi Jews had developed over centuries, and out of the many European cultures and their specific cultural environments, and had, regardless of the history, melted together with them and had created an amalgamate of excellence in the personification of artists, inventors, thinkers, and political leaders. The communication and cooperation between them were plentiful and, to a large extent, excluded the Middle Eastern and North African Jews. Most of us were recent arrivals and did not have the same level of education, following hundreds of years of colonization by the Ottoman Empire and later by Western Europe. Iraq, as a British colony, was not allowed the autonomy to rule to the benefit of its people, build schools, or invest in an infrastructure to support its own growth and prosperity.

I, like so many others from the Middle East and North Africa, was not able to envision a future for myself in Israel that would amount to anything more than a worker bee existence. The State of Israel itself had been primarily taken over by idealistic Europeans who may not have been qualified to run the country and yet were put in charge of doing so. And so, as much as I had wanted to take part in the building of the great Jewish state, I still felt like an outsider. This inability to thrive and integrate was ultimately what drove my decision to leave the country and move to the US.

At age 23, I was teaching at the Design School, studying sculpture at the Avni School of Art in Tel Aviv, a school that still exists today, and finally, falling in love. I met my first girlfriend at this time, a student my age, at the Interior Design School where I was teaching. This would turn out to be my first relationship, and it would last a full year. I will say this relationship started while I was also involved with a fellow student at the art school. I had found a way to be wanted and embraced in a community through the women in my life, and I was finally successful at attracting and winning over the competition. My life became extremely busy, between teaching during the day, art school in the evening, multiple romantic pursuits and conquests, as well as the required commutes from one place to the other, finally ending the evening at home with my mother. She waited all night for my return despite the fact that I was hardly ever home. The time when I spent the evenings with my mother seemed to be more and more a thing of the past. By now, I only saw my mother briefly when I came home late for dinner and collapsed into a deep sleep before having to rise and repeat the routine again the following morning. My personality and behavior were changing as well. I became much more self-assured and outgoing, at least much more than I had been before my newfound successes as a teacher, an artist, and a lover.

The teaching position, together with my art school experience and my personal triumphs, stoked an awakening in me. The shy boy had grown up to be a confident and content young man. The experience and pride I felt in the creative fields I pursued and my successes at the art school gave me a new and different, higher sense of self. Until then, I had felt an intellectual inferiority, not being able to dialogue fluently or, more generally, measure up to my physically larger or more educated peers. The more I learned about sculpting and the more I was able to create, the more the limitations waned, so whatever had held me back to date just melted away. This was when I realized that my future was in the Visual Arts, and the irreversible certainty formed that I was to become an artist and, at that time, a sculptor.

So many things became clearer to me. For instance, my younger sister had often imitated me in little, mundane things when we were growing up. This had annoyed me to the point that I hated her for it. Now, she could no longer torture me with her mockery, as she was not an artist. She was now living an entirely different life with a husband and children, and I had transformed, going in an entirely different direction. I grew up to be the only artist in the family, who, like the father we lost all those years ago, was actively creative and earning a living being so.

I remember the competitiveness of my youngest sibling as very painful, most likely and especially because I already, at that time, had creative ambitions and did not want to see my obvious originality hindered or mocked by a younger sibling. Today, I can better empathize with her attempts at attracting attention away from me to herself. Sibling rivalries are commonplace, and our rivalry tormented me.

After three years of Art School, I graduated in 1966 and became a sculptor while continuing to teach carpentry at the School for Art and Design. It wasn't until two years later, in 1968, that I would exhibit my work in a two-person show in Petach-Tikva, a suburban part of Tel Aviv. I exhibited my sculptures alongside a painter, and the critic's response to our show was very good. I didn't sell any of my work, but to my joy, the cultural art center that hosted the exhibit asked to retain a couple of my pieces for their permanent collection.

I slowly moved to increase my freedom and independence, sharing an apartment part-time with my friend Sam in Tel Aviv. My nights at the apartment allowed me, for the first time, the privacy to socialize with friends and love interests, away from the scrutiny of my mother and family. These were happy and carefree times that led to strengthening my relationship with Sam, who would soon after move to the US, making it easier for me to want to follow him a year later to NYC.

This wasn't the only reason I decided to move to NYC. The primary reason was that despite my now considerably improved social and professional standing in Israel, I still felt the inferiority that came from being a Middle Eastern Jew as opposed to a European one. My confidence, in fact, still ran only skin deep. I discovered, when it came to comparisons and intellectual competitiveness with Israel's elite, that I would not be able to further my artistic career as much as I desired in this environment. In essence, the

European Jews considered us part of the Israeli problem as we were a reminder of the cultures and the regions they considered to be enemy territory, both ideologically and physically. This, of course, was exacerbated by the 1967 six-day war, mainly in Sinai, which I was drafted into as well.

# Internal Conflicts

The years between 1962 and 1969 in Israel were complicated. I was too young to comprehend the times of the first Arab-Israel War, which followed the Israeli Declaration of Independence in the spring of 1948. My family had not yet arrived in Israel, and I was barely seven years old. The second Arab-Israeli War, also known as the Suez Crisis, started in October 1956. It lasted for nine days, and here, too, I wasn't mature enough to recognize the implications or true extent of the events taking place. I had just turned 16 years old, only a few years from being drafted into the Army. It was the last year of my high school education at the Technical High School, where I would graduate in Carpentry and Wood Design. It was not until the third Arab-Israeli "Six-Day War" that I was old enough to fight as a soldier between the front and the back lines. It was June 1967, and while young men from the United States fought in Vietnam, we had a short but grave and deadly war, mainly on the Sinai Peninsula. Even though I was in the Morse Code unit, I felt rather unfit for the role of a soldier. This was exacerbated by the fact that I may have been significantly younger than my fellow soldiers in my draft. I didn't know my exact date of birth, which was not out of the ordinary in the Middle East. These were trying times in our region, times of colonization and hunger.

We did not have the luxury and privilege to note the day a child was born. As a matter of fact, the birth year seemed to stand out only because it was related to other global events of the time. So, one may have known that I was born in the year of a major war or drought, and of course, relative to the other children in the family – three years after this sibling or two years before that one. My father was unusual in his dedication as he had apparently kept a prayer book where he estimated our birth dates. The book, however, was not terribly precise and was further complicated by the fact that it was based on the Jewish calendar. The Jewish or Hebrew Calendar is a lunisolar calendar system going back to the time of the Babylonian empire.

The present Hebrew calendar is the result of a process of development that includes the Babylonian influence. Until the Tannaitic Period (approximately 10-220 CE), the calendar employed a new crescent moon, with an additional month normally added every two or three years to correct for the difference between the lunar year of twelve lunar months and the solar year. The year in which it was added was based on the observation of natural agriculture-related events in ancient Israel. So, even though my father wrote what he believed was the year and month, and perhaps even the date of our birthdays to the best of his knowledge, these were often inaccurate estimates. There were no actual documents or proof of our birth dates. Our Israeli identification documents reflected what we estimated to the immigration authorities upon arrival at the refugee camp. The official Israeli calendar was the Christian Calendar, and we had to convert our approximate birthdays, months, and years into the universal Christian Calendar. To add to the confusion, my father had purposefully aged all the members of our family, believing that would qualify us for a larger tent or more subsidies while we were held in the camp.

# The Trauma of War

As a reservist, now about 26 years old, I was drafted in my capacity as a Morse Decoder, liaising between the commander and a doctor in the field who was treating the wounded soldiers from the frontlines. This experience, even though during a relatively short period, affected me gravely and lastingly, well past my years in Israel. I remember riding in a tank with the doctor and the driver between the front lines, responding to the wounded soldiers and dealing with the bodies of the dead. I was in the tank with the doctor when he was shot and met his death immediately. After the doctor's death, his driver and I were assigned the task of collecting the bodies of Israeli soldiers – both the injured and dead – and carrying them back to the field hospital up to five miles from the scene of the battle.

I cannot erase from my memory the stench of the dead or the sight of the bloated bodies scattered in the desert. The entire area reeked of death – a sweet, pungent, and repulsive smell that triggered one's reflex to vomit and overwhelmed all senses. Even worse was the sight of the decomposing bodies, which happened rather quickly in the ferocious June heat of the desert. Swollen with the gases that rapidly developed, the dead soon lost all former human semblance, and while still lying in the field and on the battleground, they turned into cartoon-like characters, swollen to balloons while still wearing their bursting uniforms, devoid of all human features. The worst, however, were the numbers. While, in comparison, a relatively small number of Israeli soldiers died during this excruciating period of war, the numbers on the other side, those of the Arab countries, were quite different and horrendous. In the six-day war, combat was the heaviest, with the most casualties on the Sinai Peninsula, where I was deployed. Israel, in its clear and resounding victory, also captured the Golan Heights from Syria, the West Bank (including East Jerusalem), the Gaza Strip, and the Sinai Peninsula. In the end, Israel's overall casualty count was around 700; however, there were more than 4,000 wounded, as compared with Israel's Arab neighbors, spearheaded by the Egyptian-Syrian Alliance, who had far more than 20,000 casualties and an undisclosed number of wounded.

# Tribe of One

Some context: The six-day war changed the status of the territories Sinai Peninsula, Gaza Strip, West Bank, Old City of Jerusalem, and Golan Heights and subsequently became a major point of contention in the Arab-Israeli conflict. Prior to the start of the war, attacks conducted against Israel by fledgling Palestinian guerrilla groups based in Syria, Lebanon, and Jordan had increased and were answered by costly Israeli reprisals. Israel's strong military showing and a smoldering territorial conflict on the Sinai Peninsula between Egypt and Israel involving the Suez Canal intensified the conflict. This caused a mobilization by the surrounding Arab States. In response to the apparent mobilization of its Arab neighbors, early on the morning of June 5th, Israel staged a sudden pre-emptive air assault that destroyed more than 90% of Egypt's air force on the tarmac. A similar air assault incapacitated the Syrian air force. Without cover from the air, the Egyptian army was left vulnerable to attack. Within three days, the Israelis had achieved an overwhelming victory on the ground, capturing the Gaza Strip and all of the Sinai Peninsula up to the east bank of the Suez Canal. During the short-ground war, while Israeli soldiers were as quickly as possible removed and tended to, a vast number of their enemy counterparts on the battlefield were left to die in the desert. As a result, an overwhelming and disproportionate number, thousands of enemy bodies, were left on the field. No one came to pick them up, at least not fast enough, neither the dead nor the wounded. There were inflated bodies strewn all over the desert that one could almost imagine them airborne, floating over the land. Eventually, these bodies were bulldozed into mass graves.

# Return From the Ashes

When I returned from the war, covered by the white dust of the desert in a soiled uniform, bearing a gun, my mother barely recognized me. My older brother had not gone to the war; he was already considered to be too old for combat and was instead assigned to a city patrol unit. Luckily, my sisters were spared as well. Women actively participated in the Israeli army, but as soldiers, they were not drafted to active combat zones or the frontlines. Unlike many of my fellow soldiers, I did not romanticize the idea of myself as a hero in fatigues, yielding a weapon and inflicting pain. I could not see anything heroic in the act of butchering people, even if they were enemy soldiers, and couldn't bear the suffering, although as a Morse coder, I was never directly involved in combat. While most of the other soldiers cheered to be in combat and proudly thought of themselves as heroes, especially after Israel's decisive victory, I never considered myself a heroic person. As a matter of fact, I always shied away from the arrogance and ego that came with holding center stage. War, by its nature, was tragic and absurd.

By the end of the war, I had become very frustrated with the State of Israel. While I was on active duty, after its conclusion, the Israelis were assessing the war and their victory, visiting the war zones and the occupied Arab territories. The Israeli population – not just the soldiers – were rejoicing and celebrating the victory over their Arab neighbors, the occupation of the former Arab territories, and the expansion of "their" promised land. They were taking pictures and filming everywhere – in the Gaza Strip, on the Golan Heights, in Sinai, and above all, in the newly gained part of the Holy City of East Jerusalem. There were depictions of victorious soldiers on army vehicles with guns in their hands and jubilant Israeli populations everywhere.

I didn't feel like rejoicing. I saw images of occupied populations traumatized and in despair in the newly gained territories. And the longer Israel occupied these territories, the more the disenfranchisement of Israel's newly added Arab population became blatantly and painfully obvious to me. That's when I realized that I could not stay in Israel for the rest of my life. At first, I didn't know where to go, but I was certain I would not continue to live there and would try to find a way to leave Israel and all this behind me.

A couple of years after that war, I resented the violence the region had gotten entrenched in, and I turned to communism for reprieve. That wasn't enough, and I decided it was time to pursue a more stable and peaceful existence. For my art, I chose to relocate to the US, knowing little more about it than what I had consumed in the handful of American movies that made their way to local theaters. New York was the natural choice, being the country's art center and where Sam, the only person I knew in the US, lived.

It was a couple of years after my arrival in NYC that I met and befriended a psychiatrist who, upon learning of my PTSD and chronic nightmares, offered to barter therapy sessions for my art. The war had left an indelible mark on me, and I needed to heal from it, but I did not know how to forget it. War is a difficult experience to overcome. The unimaginable cruelty and absurdity of the war changed me in every way.

# Looking Back

*"To an absurd mind reason is useless and there is nothing beyond reason. The absurd man, on the other hand, does not undertake such a leveling process. He recognizes the struggle, does not absolutely scorn reason, and admits the irrational. Thus he again embraces in a single glance all his experiences and is inclined to leap without sufficient thought. He knows simply that in that alert awareness there is no further place for hope"*

**—*Albert Camus, The Myth of Sisyphus***

My years in Israel were difficult, especially as I was coming of age and bearing the weight of my foreignness and insecurities. This was especially difficult for me because I wanted, more than anything else, to be the master of my mortal destiny, as I would eventually become in the US. Those early years of youth were vastly illuminating, as it was this suffering that informed my awareness and understanding of who I was and what I might become. The feeling and, later, acceptance of being different from those around me necessitated that I take the risk to change my situation. I moved to the US out of necessity – not so much for financially ambitious reasons, but rather out of a creative necessity. My survival instinct was what willed me to keep pursuing a better fate despite my otherness and foreignness.

Then and now, my self-acceptance and awareness are deeply rooted in the first 30 years of my life, having been forced to flee my first home, Iraq, and later, choosing to leave my second home, Israel.

Arriving in New York in 1969, I was once again on a new search for both a metaphysical home as well as a concrete place in which I could set roots. Today, after 50 years of calling NYC home, fathering two adult children, and being an accomplished artist and husband, my pursuit of this continues.

The passage of time doesn't seem to have dampened my gypsy soul. Immigrating meant a new uprooting, whether voluntary or an escape from deprivation or war. Every person who immigrates flees one thing and seeks another, always at the expense of loved ones and former selves,

## Tribe of One

seeking a more fulfilling fate elsewhere – reinvention in the pursuit of happiness, as in the American constitution.

# Early Seduction

In Greek Mythology, there are many examples of female seduction, incestuous and otherwise. Leaping forward into the modern/contemporary discourse and into a more sanitized world, most seductions are ascribed to men over women, fathers and daughters, uncles and nieces, and so on. The seduction of sons by their mothers doesn't seem to warrant the same amount of interest and attention. It is arguably one of the most overlooked incidents and relationships in child development. Patriarchy has a lot to do with it. As we look at a patriarchal world, we see sons coveting mothers from a patriarchal point of view. We see them longing for the other sex, mirroring their fathers, uncles, and others. I have not encountered it described from the perspective of the overbearing matriarch, the devouring female that bears down on her young and helpless son.

I grew up surrounded by many a sister and aunt. My only brother was about 15 years older than I was, so he was, especially as the oldest child, more of a father figure to me. When my father died, my older brother naturally stepped in to fill his role and duties, providing for the family as the head of the household. So, from the young age of about ten, I only saw my brother as a responsible adult rather than a mere sibling. I was equally coddled by my four older sisters, who focused their energies on preserving and protecting me.

My mother was still mourning the loss of her second son when she gave birth to me. My slightly older brother had died only a few months after birth. The more my parents were excited about the arrival of another son, who had the promise of replacing the other, the more my role became the replacement for the lost son.

This led to a rather unique setup in our family as I was destined to become the pet brother for my five older siblings and my mother. My younger, menacing sister played a different role in my upbringing; I will get to that later.

I was a small child growing up, and the fact that I was pampered by my sisters and my mother without a male role model did not give me the confidence and grit of a tough guy. Strength is what was considered manly in the world I grew up in. My mother and my sisters, however, seemed to enjoy the fact that I was small, slight, and vulnerable. They loved pampering me without sparing any opportunity to tease me.

As I was the only "male" around my mother, she brought me along to many of her own social activities. I joined her and my sisters at the all-women Hamam (public baths), and I shared my sisters 'bedroom, which was not commonplace in Iraqi culture.

I remember my visits with my mother to the *hamam*, the Arabic steam bath house in Iraq, from as early as age five. All Iraqis, regardless of faith, shared the weekly ritual of visiting the public baths for a deep scrub and massage. Only the most affluent homes had running water and the facilities to run a bath at home. For the rest of us, the public baths were one of the quotidian activities of the time. The nakedness of the large and hairy women haunted me at the time. I didn't see any beauty or seduction in those encounters. Their large, voluptuous bodies and hairy bushes were not something I coveted or appreciated. Rather, it felt like a weird, demonstrative, monstrous display of female flesh, sexuality, and power. In a hamam, where the genders were divided into separate sections, I had the misfortune of being small enough to pass for a boy young enough to enter the women's hamam. There, one is, in principle, washed, massaged, and scrubbed clean by professionals, no different from spas today.

Multiple stages followed, in rooms where one would continue washing oneself and then proceed to relax naked on the hot marble slabs, similar to a sauna. Since I was a boy in the women's hamam with my mother, I had to be washed and touched by the women who were in charge of it, and who, to me, seemed enormous and harsh. They scrubbed my skin with all their strength despite my pleas and clear discomfort with their rigor. It was intended as a luxury at the time, paying someone to slough the dead skin off and massage your body, but to me, it was a haunting experience. The women laughed loudly and pummeled me with their large breasts as they went about their work on me. I feared that they would suffocate me at times. I still remember it all vividly, despite the years since, and it is perhaps still the cause of a lot of anxiety that occasionally overcomes me in my encounters with the opposite sex.

At home, my sisters teased me ferociously, and so did their female friends. I remember one in particular, Carmella, who came to visit my older sister often. She was already fully developed, with a big bosom, and loved to lean over and press my small head and face into her chest. From my perspective, she did it on purpose and enjoyed both my embarrassment and clear excitement.

Doing the forbidden – flirting and exploring our boundaries – became a game between me and my sisters, one that they encouraged and initiated. I started watching my sisters getting dressed and undressed and became more and more interested in personal female matters, their sexuality, and physique. I would cover my head under the blanket and let my eyes follow them around our room, going on with their morning and evening routines. Sharing the same room gave me plenty of opportunity to indulge in this activity.

Carmella eventually became my first love interest at the very young age of ten years old. I remember her scent to this day and how much her touch aroused me. She kissed me on my mouth, laughed and teased me, and I reveled in the attention and softness of her body. I would lie awake at night fantasizing about her body and touch. It would arouse me, and this was when I started masturbating to my fantasies of her. I can say with confidence, and after all these years of remembering her so vividly, that she was my first love.

Being surrounded by female bodies at such an early age and in that otherwise conservative environment is what most likely drove my lifelong interest in the naked female body. Even when I had girlfriends, or later, when I was married, I continued to be enamored and stimulated by the diversity of live models who, to this day, serve as the inspiration for my paint and sculpture.

My earliest years in the harem that was my childhood home shaped my interest in everything female in a very specific way. I became obsessed with the female body that had ceaselessly teased me when I was a young boy and that had come to define me as a young man. These formative years, with very little contact with the male role models or activities, meant that I could relate to women much more. Today, so much later in life, I seek the company of women still, whether at a birthday party for my grandchild or with female therapists. I unconsciously drift to the female gaze and pursue their company, whether socially or professionally. And even though I can still conjure up the feelings and sensations of being partially violated by my older siblings and their friends or my visits to the hamam with my mother, I feel drawn to women and their bodies in a very observant and oddly trusting way.

*"The toothed vagina is no sexist hallucination: every penis is made less in every vagina, just as mankind, male and female, is devoured by mother nature."*

—Camille Paglia, Sexual Personae, 1991

## Challenges and Confrontations

My time in the army only served to make my inferior status in the pecking order. The army, for most of the young men at that time, had a glamorous appeal. It was an honor to join the Israeli Forces, a new army with the promise to defend and preserve Israel. For me, though, the way it presented itself, the army was a gauntlet walk as I continued to feel alienated from my community. I was months shy of my tenth birthday when my family arrived in Israel in 1949, and from then on, the road to adolescence was paved with challenges. The challenges we confronted were typical to recent immigrants, particularly those of Middle Eastern descent. These were a reflection of the conflicting social struggles shaping what was to become the new society. Israel was struggling with the integration of its diverse members, more so with the newer immigrants from anywhere other than the favored Central and Eastern Europeans. As my family worked to integrate, we found that our new country needed to value the skills we brought, like being a goldsmith, watchmaker, jeweler, or banker. These were the professions the Iraqi Jews were particularly good at, and they were not yet deemed a necessity in a nascent country still taking shape.

Coming of age without a father figure or male role model, I neither recognized the world I was growing up in nor did I have a guiding hand in how to behave or to persevere in it. There I arrived, at the end of high school, without the faintest idea of what I wanted to make of myself in this life. With no experience in budding manly matters, from the simple interactions with other men or fellow classmates to the first romantic experiences with the other sex, I was still a book with empty pages. When my naivete and innocence were disrupted with my being drafted into the Israeli army at the age of 18, my notions of glamorous beginnings in the Army soon gave way to the realization that this was only a continuation of my inferior status quo. The experience served to solidify my place as the outsider who didn't fit in and affirm my self-perceived shortcomings, from my height to my delicate physique to my insufficient language skills. I lacked the macho attitude and brazen language that seemed to be required to become what was then considered a hero soldier. The army coveted those who resembled a US Army

Seal. These were the chosen few who would be destined to become Israeli Army Paratroopers, the most coveted army education. Even though I wanted to be trained as a pilot, I soon learned that I was not made out of the stuff it takes to be granted an education as a pilot, as I was practically and rudely told I could not muster it. This condemnation essentially declared that even if I had passed the physical exams, I, in the opinion of my superiors, would not have been able to pass the required written and verbal exams. Instead, I was assigned to the Morse Code interpretation school, as Iraqi Jews were stereotyped as skilled at mathematics and not much else.

This meant that I, in principle, had become one of the servicemen and women who remained behind the scenes, serving the active combatants rather than operating directly on the front lines. My years serving in the army were not so much of a heroic experience as much as just turning me into an army worker bee that was mostly confined to secondary army tasks.

## Pursuing a Compromise

At the age of 21, unsure of what to do with my life after my years in the service, I actively started searching for a vocation that could define who I was able to become.

My network was comprised of my high school teachers, so I turned to them. A kind teacher of Czech descent gave me my first job assisting him in his architecture firm in Tel Aviv. This apprenticeship was where I first learned to draw and draft architectural designs for both commercial and residential spaces. It was a small office with just the seven of us, and I was the most junior apprentice. The bulk of my duties entailed replicating the architectural designs after they were rendered by my colleagues to create additional drafts of these. This was an essential task so the engineers could execute our designs, but I found it dull. The hours were long, and as I did not earn enough to move out of my mother's house, the job also required a long and arduous commute to and from my home in the suburbs. It was then that I realized I had the ambition to be more than someone's apprentice or assistant and that I had to do something of my own. I was grateful for this opportunity, but I could not stick around for much longer.

That desire further affirmed my intuition that I was destined to create with my hands, leveraging my instincts and imagination. In my search for a way out of this, my new beginning came to me in the hallways of the art school in Tel Aviv. It was the only one I could find, and the decision was obvious. Upon enquiring, I found that their admission requirements included passing a string of interviews with various professors on the subject of art. My first task was to read all the art books I could get my hands on, so I started frequenting the libraries of Tel Aviv to prepare for these interviews. Their requirements for a portfolio were what got me sketching with charcoal. What had started as a childhood hobby developed into cubist and geometric renderings based on the work I had been doing during my apprenticeship at the architecture firm.

When I was assured of my acceptance at the art school, I resigned from my apprenticeship and started to pursue other jobs to support myself and my mother. A newspaper advertisement brought me to teach architecture at a public women's college, which upskilled and trained female cadets returning from army service. This job better satisfied my secret desires for autonomy and leadership. It also conveniently placed me in a female-dominated environment, overseeing and driving the development of my students. I was also earning considerably more than I had until then.

Attending the art school the following fall, I was finally surrounded by peers who were closer to me in nature and spirit. Our physical dominance did not matter, and our introversion was not perceived as a hindrance. Rather, the inherent sensitivity that came with being an artist was revered and nurtured, for once, a positive attribute. Amongst my fellow art students, we were the Anti-Hero, and that set us apart, for once, as an advantage that earned us accolades and attracted the attention of the young women we encountered. For me, the power to attract had a wide audience: my students in my daytime job and my female artist colleagues.

The attention I received from these young women made me more self-confident, and I finally experienced my first romantic and sexual encounters. This opened up a whole new world for me, and I enjoyed it to the fullest extent. Working for the first time with live models in class, I could once again see a fully unclothed young woman, standing, at times, with her hips thrust out and always simply naked in plain sight. Unlike the women of the hamams of my childhood, these nude women inspired and motivated me in every way. Each one was a muse and a joy to gaze upon, paint, and imagine in various states.

These were tremendously joyous experiences and a great relief in countering my earliest impressions of the female body when my mother took me to the Hamams. Here, the graceful nudes had beautiful rosy or tan skin. Their curves were distinguishable and distinguished. No overlapping folds of flesh or sagging skin, no violent movements or loud laughs, just a soft serenity enveloping the room as we artists painted our visions of their beauty. We had male models as well, of course, and I was only drawn to the female body, studying it most intently and cherishing these moments, for I had craved them for what seemed to be an eternity. This fascination with the female body and my love for it has only grown since. It is a hunger I have yet to satisfy, and I hope that I never will. This constant thread through the various stages of my art and life. What had started almost violently, like so much else in my childhood, was now a source of pleasure, passion, and beauty in my art and in my daily life. My encounters with the muse intrigued me and nurtured my creativity, finally giving me the connection and belonging to my inner sanctuary.

## From Guilt to Attention

As I settled into my new life in NYC, I continued to mature and grow into my new self. I was a late bloomer in so many ways, having come to understand my true motivations and desires as I came of age in my years of service in the Israeli Army. I began to claim my independence with my decision to become an artist and attend the Art School of Tel Aviv in my late 20s. Later, in my 30s, having arrived in New York, I kept moving closer to my fuller vision of who I wanted to be. I pursued my deepest desires, be it in my art, my life, or, more specifically, my sexuality.

Finally, I became independent and freed from the burden of my mother's need for my time and attention and the guilt that came along with it. What came with this, of course, was an ocean of loneliness. Again, re-learning the local language, rebuilding community through friends, and relevance in my vocation and the art world. The lightness of my newfound freedom was dampened by the familiar fears of acceptance and inferiority. As I had in my youth, I once again withdrew into my shy, protective shell and tried to silence the doubtful voices in my head. Had I really made the best choice by leaving Israel and turning my back on what was familiar until that time? I could still vividly remember my irrelevance and the struggles of my past. Failing was not an option, and returning was not going to allow me to move forward. I had to throw myself into building this new life and making NYC my own. The price was going to be steep, but it was all or nothing, and I had to take the risks and hope I would be rewarded with the things I wanted for myself – a family, a home, and respect in my new community. My frustration with the familiarity of this predicament only added to my anxieties and made it harder for me to go out into this new reality.

My life had been determined by so many external factors; for example, my family deciding to relocate to Israel and my siblings caring for me as they supported the family following my father's passing. My friends, and eventually roommates. Then, of course, the girlfriends I had.

This, at first, may come as a surprise, but for me, these individual relationships were such a steering force. They had a much bigger influence on me than on others because of the age gap between my siblings and me and the absence of engaged parents. My father passed so young, and my mother was never able to adapt and acclimate to our new life in Israel.

This was further exacerbated by my introverted nature and my longing for the warmth and protection of the family. I preferred and pursued the depth of individual relationships and found these easiest to create with women whom I loved or craved and relied on to alleviate my loneliness and fears. So, they became my source of comfort and security, the closest replica of a nuclear family structure of two. Their acceptance fulfilled my need to be desired and silenced my fears of failure. That didn't mean I was always dedicated to one sexual partner. These were the early 70s, and by today's standards, I was part of a generally promiscuous generation. Having sex was not uniquely reserved for monogamous relationships. One could be dedicated to one person and still pursue casual sexual relationships outside of that relationship. All was very free and casual; having sex with someone was often preceded by going out to dinner or going dancing. It was part of the social discourse between men and women, women and women, and men and men.

I engaged in these norms in NYC and recognized in them some of the physical gestures of love that I had witnessed growing up. Platonic relationships included my brother holding hands with his best guy friend and my sisters washing one another and laying closely in bed with their girlfriends. This, I think, helped me embrace the times. I didn't see our open sexuality as a foreign taboo or barrier to friendship, for that matter. It was merely an extension of the pleasure of touch and intimacy with those we trusted and loved.

That free-spirited love was true of my partners as well, such as Susan, my first love and live-in partner of two years upon arriving in 1970s New York. It was also the case with Maria, the exotic dancer I lived with next. We were so close that we traveled together back to Israel, where she met my family, who adored her, to say the least.

The next big chapter of my life opened when I met Sarah Amos, a young "Au Pair" from England. Sarah had come to stay with a family of intellectuals and classical music lovers, the head of the family having been a musical conductor. I met her through a mutual friend. What started as a curious conversation between strangers quickly turned into a mutual and passionate attraction. She was stunning, and we didn't waste too much time before we moved in together. She was tall and slim, with extraordinarily fair skin and beautiful blonde hair. Her unusual height was a striking contrast to my stout figure, as was her exceptional beauty and sophistication. Despite that and the bemused looks we garnered from strangers in public, I felt very assured and confident with her. We cared for one another deeply and bonded over our adventures and explorations of our new home, NYC. We were a pair of beginners in a new world we were eager to explore – while being frightened by it as well. Sarah was also a trained goldsmith, and this endeared further, taking me back to my father's profession as a goldsmith and his love for the art of jewelry making.

We thoroughly enjoyed our time together, talked and laughed a lot, and had many adventures in the big new city. However, we both struggled financially to make ends meet. She, at times, brought food home from the family she worked for, which we hungrily consumed and were grateful for. At the time, wine and drugs were easy to come by, and we often went to parties for the sole purpose of eating, drinking, and getting high.

Other times, we went shoplifting at a supermarket, grabbing expensive cheeses, foie gras, or other artisanal high-end foods that we could find unattended. We would hurry home, pockets and sleeves stuffed with our sustenance, feeling privileged and on top of the world with the adrenaline from breaking the rules and getting away with it. The adrenaline sustained us and kept us going back.

This went on for months until, one day, we got caught in one of the stores. They brought us to the back office and made it clear that if we were to get caught shoplifting again, the repercussions would be grave, and the police would be involved. This was especially alarming to me as a new immigrant and more so to Sarah, who, by now, was on an expired au pair visa, deeming her status illegal. I had initiated my citizenship application, and this would create issues I did not want to contemplate. Sarah would have most likely been deported had we been caught and reported to the police.

Sarah, much younger than I at the time, was struggling with defining her identity, even more so than I was with defining mine. We didn't socialize much outside of my immediate art community, which at that time presented itself as often contemplative, depressed, and withdrawn, fueled by intellectual books, drugs, music, new age, or meditation practices. It was a lifestyle that generally ignored sports or anything healthy and wholesome. I, in comparison to Sarah, felt more comfortable with our environment and circumstances. The art circle was my own, and she hung on the periphery, not able to engage with us. She awkwardly lingered in the background when we socialized, withdrawing into her own thoughts while I enjoyed the company of my fellow artist friends. I felt the pressure of her silence and seeming melancholy, unable to assert herself within our boisterous and excitable crowd. Her silence made me uncomfortable. Her beauty attracted everyone's attention, and none of my friends 'efforts to engage her succeeded.

Sexually, we were very good together. Despite the height difference, we satisfied one another's hunger and never minded the stares we elicited in public. We were an uncommon couple, and our exoticism to one another was a huge part of our attraction. The height difference, the contrasting mix of the attributes of a fair and blonde, tall woman uniting with a darker skinned, hairy, stout man, makes, by all standards, a perfect coupling of opposites attracting.

Now, this may sound like a fantastic racial stereotype – most prominent in fairy tales, if you read between the lines, openly alluding to it in Rumpelstiltskin. For whatever unexplained reason, Rumpelstiltskin wanted to have a child from a tall, fair beauty in exchange for his services, the spinning of gold. I grew up in the Middle East, a world where women were mostly covered. Husbands and wives in the most conservative of families may not have even seen one another completely unclothed. Male jealousy was part of the inherent mentality and a trademark of male chauvinism and machismo, yet I did not feel this jealousy when I was with my female partners. This was true of my very close relationship with Sarah at that time, despite her other sexual encounters, which did not amount to anything comparable to ours in depth or intimacy. I also exercised the benefits of our open relationship. This was perhaps the difference in our times during the early 1970s.

We overcame the myriad of barriers and built a dedicated, adventurous, humorous, poetic, sexual, and otherwise creative relationship that rose above the other. We stayed together for two years, sharing things we loved from our past, like recipes from our native backgrounds. Sarah showed me how to make her specialty Yorkshire pudding, her childhood favorite, or curry, which was influenced by the people from India who had migrated to her home country, England, etc. She taught me about spices I had never tasted, and I, in turn, showed her how to make some of the Iraqi dishes I grew up with.

We even started considering getting married. The fact was, she was illegal now, and I had already obtained a Green Card by then and was well on my way to American citizenship. I thought marrying her would help her find a legal way to stay in the country. Then, we visited a friend of mine, Leon Smith, in Hudson, and I told him about our plans. He strongly discouraged us from doing so. We were both struggling financially, barely getting by and we, ourselves, were questioning our ability to support one another and earn a comfortable enough living together. The challenges we faced were difficult to bear, and we were now testing the relationship and pushing ourselves apart. We each wanted more for ourselves, and our appreciation of one another and love could not sustain our bond for much longer.

# Concept to Conceptual

The New York art scene was a double-edged sword, presenting lots of opportunities and pitfalls as well. Unlike in Israel, where artists were still focused on the creation of modern (avant-garde) art and where I could revel in the joy of painting real models, in 1970s New York, the most revered art reflected conceptual ideas. The most popular works were largely non-representational, minimalist, mixed-media, and ephemeral – primarily concept-driven works. Found objects were being incorporated into the artworks, and there seemed to be a boundless freedom to use whatever materials one dared incorporate. This was a significant change from the classic era traditions preceding these times when artists primarily leveraged oil or acrylic to paint and natural materials, like bronze, wood, or marble, in three-dimensional art. Of course, the conceptual artworks were primarily those of Ivy League-educated elites, with a few notable exceptions. The NYC scene was also introducing to the world the idea of pop art, and in this arena, the likes of Andy Warhol, Robert Rauschenberg, and Roy Lichtenstein reigned supreme and were primarily represented and marketed by the Leo Castelli Gallery in SoHo.

The New York art world in downtown Manhattan was also predominantly white male American and, to some extent, European. There were a few exceptions, as is always the case, the most prominent of which was Jean-Michel Basquiat, who exploded on the scene later in the 1980s. New York's creativity was booming in those years. It wasn't just the visual artists who were at the center of creativity and creation; there were also many actors, dancers, composers, and musicians in the downtown art world of those days. The SoHo neighborhood (South of Houston) had become a hub for the country's creatives, with artist studios and rehearsal spaces taking over the downtown real estate. This deemed SoHo a global powerhouse of creativity and a magnet to the outside world.

My first studio was on Crosby Street, right in the heart of SoHo, immediately north of Chinatown, in an empty commercial building full of artist studios. This downtown community's needs were powerfully served by a cheap local rag named The Village Voice. It was the guide to everything that could matter to these artists. It was in this paper's pages that I replied to an advertisement placed by an artist looking for a roommate to share his loft and the rent.

Despite the zoning of these lofts as commercial, we struggling artists inhabited them full-time and made them our homes, albeit illegally. Eventually, the New York Loft Laws caught up with the times and allowed to live and work in these spaces.

The space we shared was large and divided into two separate and distinct sections. My roommate, Robert Grovesner, worked from his space and went home to his wife at the end of the day. I, on the other hand, struggled to make ends meet, but I worked and lived in the space, sharing it with Sarah during the time we were together. When we separated, she didn't move far, finding a space a short walking distance away on Mulberry Street.

The other powerful NY institutions at the time were the local mafia, primarily Italian or Jewish. They ruled downtown NYC with an iron fist and owned most of the real estate. Racism and discrimination were rampant at the time, and these gangs were biased toward us artists, sometimes even offering us rent reductions, only to keep us, artists, in place and keep out potential tenants from poorer communities. Downtown NYC real estate was not as valuable then as it later became. These properties were mostly in shabby condition and were only useful as commercial properties, like warehouses and factories. As the industry moved out of NYC, the artists moved into these spaces without much competition from anyone else. SoHo streets, in those days, were dark, dirty, and mostly dangerous. Waste collection was infrequent, street lights did not exist, and the sound of gunshots was no surprise.

By the end of the 1970s, SoHo, like much of NYC, had sufficiently gentrified, and many of these buildings had changed ownership. As new landlords took over, they, in many cases, did their best to evict the artist tenants so they could list these spaces at the higher going market rates. I was eventually evicted from that first Crosby Street Studio, but that was not until much later.

SoHo's mix of artist residents included poets, writers, and even small publishers. I still had not received a formal language education, and so continued my inability to engage in complex conversations beyond the quotidian. Without adequate cultural references to serve as a foundation, I could barely grasp what they were writing about. I was similarly challenged by the work of the "art and language" community. I frequently found myself lost and bored with the discourse that only a small number of artists were so steeped in. This school included conceptual artists like Lawrence Weiner, Joseph Kosuth, and Jenny Holzer, whose work was primarily based on words and language.

Despite this small circle of artists, the SoHo art scene was most prominently shaped by a group of Ivy League graduates, including the conceptual, minimalist artists Richard Sierra and Chuck Close. They dominated the downtown art scene and were making names for themselves that were far beyond city limits. They were on their way to become the stars of their generation.

In this era, the most coveted works were of the Minimalist, Conceptual, or Pop Art schools. Pop Art, which had ruled the art scene well before the other two, was the more mature of this group. It was a very American movement that required knowledge and sensitive handling of the American cultural iconography and way of life. Minimalism, as well as conceptualism, emerged in different parts of the world, not entirely simultaneously, and while not rooted in America, NYC was the hotbed of inspiration in those years and where much of this art was taking shape. These schools often strongly connected with references to the artists' native or chosen countries. Artists like Joseph Kosuth, Nam June Paik, and Lee Ufan went on to influence this scene from their adopted home, NYC.

Neither the city nor the art scene proved as easy for me to navigate. Conceptual art, for instance, required that the artist express the inspiration and message of the work, which, with my limited language skills, was difficult to communicate in English. It seemed that despite my efforts to pursue this conceptual art, I remained rooted in my point of reference – the human figure, or more specifically, the female form.

All this was happening in an environment where art was pursued for its sake rather than its commercial viability. It was, in fact, a matter of pride. Emphasizing one's vision and creativity, without commercial merit, was considered passion for one's art – a belief and commitment in one's lofty ideals, along with the overarching interpretation of the work.

Needless to say, I continued to feel foreign, no matter how much I learned and what chasms I closed. My art had developed, but I was still supporting myself with other odd jobs, driving taxis, and whatever else I could find. Selling my art was a necessity to me, and its commercial value was an imperative need to be able to survive with dignity and pride in my work. I could not afford to turn my nose to the idea that creating art was alone the goal. This was a stark contrast to the artist graduates of Yale, or RISD, or the parallel art circle formed by the well-established European powerhouses like Arman or Christo, who, despite relocating to NYC, were able to expand their success and influence, without the challenges confounding other new immigrants like myself. They, in fact, went on to become even more powerful in the art world after adopting NYC as their new home.

## Driving a Taxi

Driving the taxi was very hard work for me. It took up my nights, following long days of assisting my art teacher and others. The streets of NYC were as foreign to me as the English language itself.

If you have seen Night on Earth by Jim Jarmusch (1991), you might get a sense of what I mean. Jim's Jarmusch portrait of NYC in the 1990s was a mere sliver of what transpired throughout a night in the 1970s. It was the most difficult task I have ever taken on, and I needed it to make a living. There were humorous encounters and episodes with the city's eccentrics, as they owned the night, reminding me today of La Cage aux Folles by Edouard Molinaro (1978) and the later American version of Bird Cage by Mike Nichols (1996). It was much darker than all the narratives I have seen of it on the screen. The closest to its stark reality came in Paul Schrader's iconic film TAXI DRIVER (1976). Paul Schrader, in an interview, once explained his intention to create a protagonist who, in his own words, would be "a brother to Albert Camus' Meursault in The Stranger or Dostojevski's Underground Man." The latter was staged in 1975 at the height of crime and corruption in New York City, during the aftermath of the Vietnam War. The story centers around a Vietnam Veteran who can barely navigate a world he becomes so detached from while driving a taxi in NYC at night.

Alienation and fear were both cab drivers' bed-fellows; they became the occupational hazard all drivers accepted then and for many years to come. The movie's narration was not, in my experience, an exaggeration. In the 1970s, in New York City, everyone struggled to survive. Many young women, especially newer immigrants, who at the time hailed from Eastern Europe, worked as escorts, prostitutes, or exotic dancers to survive. These were the circumstances of Maria, my second major relationship – having newly arrived from Croatia. The men, especially in Downtown Manhattan, many of them artists and creatives more generally, turned to driving taxis to support themselves. The taxis usually belonged to a taxi company that was, if not literally, run like a mafia organization.

## Tribe of One

I had no money and no marketable skills. Driving a taxi was difficult in NYC as I didn't know the city or its boroughs and was not fluent in English. Despite this, I got the job and worked hard to supplement my income in the City That Never Sleeps. This wasn't unique to me. Many night-shift taxi drivers were students or old Jewish men with few other options to earn a living.

All that have seen "Night On Earth" surely remember the character Helmut, a recent arrival from East Germany and a product of the great thaw between the two opposing empires, the Soviet Union and the United States. Like me, unaware of societal barriers or NYC's boroughs, neighborhoods, and dangers, he would end up lost on many of his trips. Some of these trips were harder than others, like getting lost driving someone back from John F. Kennedy airport. So lost, in fact, that the man almost assaulted me and, upon finally arriving at his destination, ran off without paying my fare.

The hours were long, and the city was dangerous, dirty, loud, and polluted. The car itself, the original checker taxi, was difficult to maneuver, heavy and large. Avoiding moving cars or pedestrians was a constant stress, and that, along with figuring out the route after picking up a passenger, was depleting. Many taxi drivers refused trips to the outer edges of the city. Neighborhoods like Harlem or Brooklyn were more dangerous than Manhattan. Sex workers used the taxis to escape police harassment or, given the large back seat, were used as a makeshift location to earn their fees. This was only matched in its audacity by the menacing encounters with the pimps. The police were another source of strife.

My nights, when they finally ended, left me with all forms of aches and frustrations. The conversations with the passengers, drunk or sober, varied between the tedious and terrifying. I was forced to listen and, worse, at times, serve advice and offer kindness to their confessions. Anything for the fee, and hopefully a tip. Late at night, the passengers were usually intoxicated or drugged out – some aggravated, and others putting me in the position of having to witness their lovemaking or lewd behavior. Some seemed to only want to get my attention or to provoke a reaction. At best, it was incomprehensible nonsense or offensive commentary on all kinds of topics depending on gender, sexual orientation, ethnicity, political or religious views. Some of the worst were the ones attempting to pay me with sexual favors in lieu of actual cash.

I had to engage with the many passengers in my taxi or risk losing tips that were crucial to sustaining my modest living. Worse than that, it also risked physical harm as some of them were prone to violence. Pimps, prostitutes, the very rich, hoodlums, or criminals who were after the cash that every driver had in their taxi also made their living during the night. It seemed most passengers came with one particular challenge or the other. I was grateful for all trips, so long as they could direct me in the direction to drive to get them to where they were going and pay me in US dollars.

At that time, around the 1970s, despite of the introduction of bullet-resistant partitions to taxi cars, there was often no effective separation between the driver and the passengers. This served to enhance the drivers 'safety and the passenger's privacy. The now common and mandatory signs in every vehicle laying out the laws protecting cab drivers from their customers, threatening fines and also incarceration in case of assaulting the driver, appeared much later. This was instated in response to many years, and violent incidents were common, whether stealing, assaulting, or, in some cases, brutally murdering the taxi driver for the cash he carries. These incidents occurred mostly in the dead of night. As a consequence, most people avoided these jobs, and there was a severe shortage of taxi drivers that were filled with new immigrants like me. To ensure this, the test requirements did not pose a significant hurdle, and we would receive our licenses to drive with little if any, knowledge of the City and its streets.

Taxi drivers fell into two categories, those desperate for second jobs in the night, like myself, or the young and fearless who had no real sense of the looming dangers, whether driving taxis or otherwise. It was not only taxis that were dangerous at that time. The City was dangerous, with a high incidence of poverty and crime. SoHo was not a place that attracted fine diners and tourists. Brooklyn had not yet gentrified into the utopia of today.

In these days of cash payments, taxi drivers ended their shifts with a large stash of cash and no effective way to protect themselves from a passenger's violent attempt to claim this. At the end of a shift, I would return the taxi car to the garage and its rightful owner, along with their daily stipend, keeping anything over and above that to myself.

Cab drivers were easy prey, and it was either for monetary gains or out of malice that they were assaulted. The Cab Drivers Protection Act was eventually implemented in 2017 to avert this (assaulting a taxi driver is punishable by up to twenty-five years in prison). This was after years of lobbying, even though the statistics showed that, for instance, in 2014, cab drivers were 25 times more likely to find a violent death at the workplace than in any other occupation. On the other hand, cab drivers did not support or protect each other in any meaningful way. Being a diverse group from varying vocations and nationalities, often with little to no language skills to communicate with one another or their passengers. Each was out to protect himself, and there was no warm chatter or common interests. Drivers competed for customers on the roads, creating dangerous situations by overtaking each other for pick-ups. It is startling that the New York Taxi Workers Alliance, a 21,000-member-strong union of New York City professional drivers, was only founded in 1998. We were also reluctant to accept ride trips to far-out locations and the outer boroughs, where some taxis would be lured to be robbed or simply stiffed on the fare.

To avoid these risks, I attempted to find a day shift, but this, alas, proved futile. Eastern European drivers had a strong hold on the day shift, being safer and more financially rewarding. I was already contemplating giving up night driving when I had what came to be one of the defining incidents of my years on that job. Towards the end of one of my shifts, just before sunrise, having picked up a drunk passenger at one of the clubs, a driver in a pick-up truck cut me off at the intersection. The older couple in the truck had missed their red light and crashed into my taxi, bringing us both to a complete halt. Our injuries were limited to minor bumps or scratches, and my passenger proceeded to exit the taxi and walk away. He did not pay me the fee quote on the taxi meter, nor did he stick around for the police to question him on events and respective roles and responsibilities in the crash. The accident shook me up, and my walking away from it safely signaled to me that it was time to change course. That morning, I returned the heavily damaged car to the garage for the last time, walking away from a perilous job I never liked nor wanted.

## Meeting at Magoo's

Magoo's, the unique TriBeCa bar, was the portal to my connection to the art world around the mid-1970s. My first visit was with Bob Grosvenor, with whom I shared the art studio on Crosby Street. After that first introduction, I felt comfortable returning, time and again, because Magoo's gave me the feeling of belonging amongst peers and other mid-career artists who, like me, struggled financially. It felt like finding my place in the art world. We each regularly experienced painful rejections from dealers and art galleries and shared these trials with one another. There was no dress code. We all arrived in our soiled jeans and t-shirts, following a long day's work at our studios, hungry for the hamburger and beer we could afford that day. Most everyone there was an artist or a musician. It was a huge and lively space with pool tables at the center of the room. Those of us who knew how to shoot pool would show off our skills at these tables. Watching this was stimulating for someone like me, having not played myself. I envied them and regretted not being able to participate in the game that people seemed to play in every bar in the city. I attempted it in a few instances and felt like it was just another thing that I could not succeed at. I eventually stopped trying. That was a recurring theme with me. When I could not compete in something, I stopped fighting it. Rather, I would give it up and busy myself with what I was able to be successful at.

Entering Magoo's with Bob gave me confidence, as he had already established himself as a respected and known abstract and minimalist sculptor. He never let anyone pin him down when it came to artistic style and managed to stay open to new ways and directions of art-making. The diversity of his work protected him from any particular artistic ideology or camp.

I shared Bob's studio for many years, and this may have been what attracted me to his orbit. He was not a sectarian operator, and his creativity was like a book with many chapters. Another thing we had in common was our foreign formative years. Many of the artists of our day and our social circle at Magoo's were American-born and educated. Bob had, like me, been shaped by the experiences of a different world when he chose to study art in Dijon and, Paris (France) and Perugia (Italy) before returning to his birthplace, NYC, to start his multi-media career. While his work evolved over his lifetime, he remained consistent and loyal, displaying his art over his 50-year career with the eponymous Paula Cooper Gallery.

I looked up to Bob as a master and a successful artist, which I was still striving to become. He was a shy person and yet was able to display aggression when required. He was admired by many at Magoo's and beyond. His adopting me as a younger artist earlier in my career gave me confidence and a sense of belonging. The other artists hanging around our table accepted me as one of them. I felt less like an outsider than ever before, and my limited language skills were, for the first time, not hindering my ability to connect. Quite the opposite, my foreign accent was now adding to my charms. Upon meeting a new person, the conversation would quickly turn to where I was from and my background. Most were fascinated with my journey, and this was one of the earliest experiences where I would be made to feel less of an outsider.

Leaving Magoo's at the end of the night, Bob would return home to his wife and children, and I would go back to my living quarters in our art studio. Here, the feelings of being alone, if not completely lonely, would push me into deep thought. What was my place and purpose in the City? Why am I here?

Magoo's was a rebellious place, untamed and rowdy, frequented by artists and creatives from all walks of life. It originated as a place for sex workers to end the night with some dinner and drink. They would socialize and, on occasion, find someone to leave with later in the night. The owner played the dual role of gatekeeper and protector of these downtrodden late-night customers. Needless to say, he was later accused of pimping, and that brought on the demise of Magoo's. The place shuttered, and the party ended in the mid-1980s.

I had to date and do what I needed to do to survive the jungle of a foreign city with no language or social skills, meeting the likes of Robert Wilson, Donald Judd, Carl Andre, George Segal, Dan Flavin, Duane Hanson as well as lesser known giants such as Yuda Ben Yehuda, Judy Rifka and the French American conceptual artist Alain Kirili.

Around this time, I felt longing for my roots and tried to find comfort in quotidian things like foods and places. This drove me to search outside of NYC, and that is when I began to spend time in Europe. Unlike the American artists, the Europeans were much more romantic and sensitive to one another. The American art world, very much in line with the general culture, was puritanical, blunt, and direct. Uncompromising with outsiders, and on many occasions, dismissive and patriotic. The Europeans emphasized the beauty of the artwork, while Americans pursued more brutal works.

By now, I had become quite ingrained in the downtown New York City art world. The French were the earliest of the Bohemians, a life style and culture they cultivated for over two centuries, and I always felt very at home in Paris, at the center of it all. I would go back and forth between France and the US, Paris, and New York, seemingly enjoying the best of both worlds and their respective art scenes. Both cities had the highest creativity levels, and the exchange between artists and other creative people was seamless. Intellectually, they were different, but not so much so that they couldn't connect, and my work flourished in this environment.

# Horace and Jaffa

I vividly recall my first visit to Horace Richter's gallery. We met in New York, though I don't exactly recall how or where. He must have encountered my work and shown interest in it, for he eventually was the first gallerist to take my latex sculptures to one of the first editions of Art Basel in Switzerland. He was also the first to show my sculptures in Israel at his gallery in the town of Old Jaffa.

The oldest part of Jaffa is nestled on a hill side South-East of Tel Aviv, overlooking the city's port on the Mediterranean Sea. The ancient Canaanite settlement was a seaside destination for pilgrims on their way to Jerusalem, and it became an Arab-majority city during the Ottoman Empire. It still bears traces of past times, layered and sedimented like palimpsests: the Crusaders, the Battle of Jaffa (112), and the Treaty of Jaffa (1229) between The Holy Empire, Richard Lionheart, and the Ottomans. It has all the traits of an age-old place with a script written in stone and blood. Today, Jaffa is an enchanting and unusual place: originally, and over the centuries, a strategic seaport outpost along the Mediterranean, it later became an art center with artist studios. It eventually developed a small but significant number of galleries for art (Horace Richter) or design, foremost by local artists such as Ilana Goor, founder of the eponymous Ilana Goor Museum in 1995 that opened to the public in 1998, in an Old Pilgrims Inn on the rocks of Jaffa overlooking the port.

Jaffa, at least in the summer, is dry and hot, smelling of ancient dust, dry earth, and old stones, only slightly softened by the breeze of the Mediterranean sea. People come out at sunset, which is when the city comes to life with hundreds of small lights behind the windows of the old town's thick walls. It has a whimsical atmosphere that almost makes one forget the history of a place that bore witness to many battles between Christians, Moslems, and Jews. Most recently, the bloodshed included the Jaffa Uprising and subsequent Riots (1921) and the Battle for Jaffa (1948).

Horace Richter's gallery itself was in the heart of the ancient town, down streets too narrow for anything other than a pedestrian or a mule. The architecture was of bygone periods with thick arched walls, many nooks, crannies, and low ceilings. Parts of the structure looked more like an ancient vault or a medieval abbey than a contemporary gallery. Horace himself was a collector who dedicated his life to his passion for contemporary avant-garde, mainly by artists from Israel or the wider Jewish diaspora.

The American critic Meyer Shapiro (also an art scholar and head of Columbia University's art department) wrote about Horace's collection in 1969 on the occasion of the Mint Museum of Art (Charlotte, NC) exhibition. Horace Richter passed away in 2006 and is remembered as a cultural catalyst within the Zionist movement. Like most, he also had critics, but nevertheless, all agreed with his love for avant-garde art and for collecting, which provided much-needed support for the contemporary artists of his era.

## Boyhood

There are many theories about what becomes of a boy who grows up with an absent father and without older male siblings or role models. In my case, raised with and by the women in my family. Some are hair-raising theories anticipating that the child, later in life, would fail to compete, persevere, or assert themselves as a worthy male partner. All of these perpetuate the myth that in order to become a man, a boy must be reared by a strong male role model. In my experience, many boys around the world are raised by women, and that alone certainly does not constitute a lack of understanding of the male child's own gender or future role in the world.

I grew up with my five sisters, and as they matured and married, was eventually left alone with my mother. This created an environment that was heavily charged with female sexuality and frequent encounters with the opposite sex from very early on in my life. The absence of male friends, created a distinct set of circumstances for me, growing up only engaging with and relating to females. I did not have male friends to play with, especially after relocating to Israel. This clearly set me apart from boys my age who had the influence of fathers, brothers, or other boys. I lost my father quite young before he and I could bond over the joys and comforts of companionship and play. My brother, significantly older than I, came of age with the burden of having to work and support our family following my father's passing. He loved me, and showed this with his hard labor, but that did not allow him the opportunity to compensate for my need for fatherly love and guidance. Their absence from my life, for different reasons, often translated to an absence of authority, masculinity and strength. The doting attention of my mother and older sisters was often deemed to have a softening effect on me, spoiling me and making me unfit. These observations might be true if we were to abide by the stereotypes that masculinity is synonymous with dominance, violence, and lack of empathy. I reject this line of thought.

I grew up playing with my older sisters and being comforted by them. They fussed over me as if I were their own child. I learned to play their games and to befriend their girlfriends. These friends reciprocated my interest sometimes and took a special liking to me.

My shyness with women was only sexual, exacerbated by the lack of interactions with women from outside of my immediate family. It was not in conflict with my attraction and desire for women and their company. Not having experienced strong bonds with men limited my ability to relate to them in a more direct or socially intimate way. This, I believe, made me seek out the company of women whether, as friends, lovers, or in my work. So much of my formative years and early development was nurtured by women. While I was later influenced by male artists, friends, or teachers, this did come later in my adulthood.

In the emotional, social, intellectual interactions, women have dominated the discourse and guided me through uncharted waters. My interest in women was never limited to sexual encounters. Rather, I craved the camaraderie, intimacy, inspiration, and understanding more than anything else. I always sought the company of women. I felt I could trust them and was therefore able to share with them my true(er) self, and seek their help and support in my times of insecurity or need. They, in turn, rewarded this, appreciating my openness and sensitive side and, at various stages of my life, providing the support and loyalty I craved.

## SoHo (South of Houston)

SoHo is the neighborhood south of Houston Street. The name originated when a few artists were looking for large spaces that were cheaper to use and in a primarily industrial area where one lived. During the Pop Art period, the artists required larger spaces to produce their work, which was typically larger in size. Since Pop Art was created from everyday life, artists such as James Rosenquist, Roy Lichtenstein, Robert Rauschenberg, and others, were at the forefront of making larger spaces the norm. The Pop Art movement prevailed during the '50s and '60s. Artists began to look for large spaces, and in NYC these were primarily in the area south of Houston Street, SoHo.

Unlike Soho in London, which was commercially designated to serve the local population and tourists, so few artists could afford spaces similar to lofts in New York City. This was the beginning of a trend that began to occur all over the world for artists and others alike, allowing them to enjoy large, mostly commercial spaces that were subsequently transformed into working/living spaces. The mentality of having a small, cozy, and romantic space was "passe" and most creatives began to enjoy the roughness and the spacious nature of the loft spaces.

I arrived from Israel, at that time, in the late 60's into a world that was foreign to me. It was a huge culture shock. Until that time, I lived with my family in a tiny one-bedroom apartment with a lavatory outside of the house. When I moved out of my family's home, I moved into a tiny room on a rooftop in Tel Aviv, where I could barely move around. There were lots of beautiful views of the sea but barely room to execute any artwork. Being introduced to loft spaces when I arrived to New York was overwhelming and intimidating. It evolved to be just as hard as not speaking or understanding the language, and the huge space added to my anxieties. I felt like a small figure thrust into a large world around me. I was searching for the *how* and *where* to progress in my new life.

Coming from the Middle East in my late 20s, never having lived in any other place, other than Bagdad, Iraq and Tel Aviv, Israel, it was all new and strange to me. The unfamiliarity of a different space, time, culture, weather,

## Tribe of One

and landscape, which was much larger than what I was accustomed to, made it very difficult for me to adjust and to accept the new reality of a different way of thinking.

In the Middle East, the climate was warmer, and in certain regions, you barely felt the winter. The heat dominated my daily life. The different climate also required an adjustment to the physicality of the buildings and landscape. I had not experienced snow on the ground or temperatures below zero. I wondered how people could live in places like that since I came from places where the weather never went below zero. I arrived at the end of October as the weather began to change from summer to fall and later on to winter. My body was acclimating to this new reality, and I felt that as my body found a new adjustment, my mind followed.

Life takes place as the weather dictates how people think, how they live, and how they relate to each other. I, having grown up in the Middle East, was accustomed to a life conducted more outside than inside, and this was formative to my thinking. Nature, as a result, dominated my creations. Needless to say, the limitation of nature manifests visibly different results.

Growing up in crowded streets in Iraq, with narrow sidewalks and merchants selling their wares outside of their homes as street vendors, working late through the night to avoid the afternoon sweltering weather. The streets were buzzing with people, talking to one another, negotiating every possible subject without a goal in mind. Bargaining was for the joy of exchanging ideas. Nobody cared about political issues since nobody could influence any change anyway. They conversed about the quotidian matters of family, work affairs, and everyday life.

There was not much wealth, so there was no competition as to who was wealthier or not. In that bazaar lifestyle, bargaining with the merchants was an honorable thing to do, and both sides, merchant, and customer, engaged in that conversation mainly to prove their knowledge about the goods being sold and bought.

Later on, as I arrived to Israel, the bargaining I was familiar with was no longer the way of life. I was beginning to experience shops as opposed to outdoor stalls. In Iraq, people sat at coffee tables on the street and talked, smoked, and drank coffee or tea. In Israel, I began to realize that cafes and restaurants opened by immigrants from Europe were primarily replicating the European lifestyle.

Upon my arrival in New York, I initially resided in Prince and West Broadway, in the center of SoHo. I lived with another two roommates in a 5,000-square-foot apartment on the top floor of the building. There was an elevator that needed to be operated manually, and the use of it required a skill to manipulate the rope that snaked through the elevator, dictating where the elevator would stop or go, and which direction it would go, up or down. There was not a practical handle for stopping or continuing movement. Grabbing the rope was the way to start the movement of the elevator. Out of fear, we mostly used the stairs in order to avoid getting stuck in the elevator. If there was a problem, we were required to call the landlord, who never responded since he barely received any rent and sometimes never received any rent at all. On such an occasion, when that happened, we would call the fire department, who came to rescue us. The concurrent fear crept in that since we were living there illegally, we would be forced to move out. We absorbed the hardship of this reality, and the landlord was happy not to be disturbed. They felt no obligation to fix the problem since that would require an expense they did not want to assume.

In the early days of SoHo, the streets were deserted and there was not street life I was accustomed to in my past. In a strange way, I enjoyed and appreciated that feeling of emptiness and anonymity. Being ignored and ignoring others gave me a feeling that everything and nothing belonged to me. The streets were full of trucks that were difficult to maneuver around. There were many workers running around doing their loading and unloading; boxes strewn all over the sidewalks, forcing us to navigate our way around. SoHo was mainly warehouses to store industrial goods such as fabric, or food supplies. Often, the trucks were blocking the streets, and often, the drivers were throwing their goods onto the sidewalk, unconcerned about pedestrians who might be walking by.

We often had to jump over materials and squeeze through loaded pallets with toppling merchandise and construction materials. The trucks would often drive onto the sidewalks and into the open warehouses to load and unload. We often had to use the streets to pass around them and always had to be wary of the other trucks passing by in order to avoid danger. By the end of the day, the streets and sidewalks were littered with leftover merchandise. Many artists at that time began to find use for these materials to create new artwork. There was a certain joy in using the material I found without having to pay for it.

At some point, this concept formed the beginning of Arte Povera, a movement that took place in the 60s through the 70s. The phrase Arte Povera is the Italian phrase for "poor art" or "impoverished art." It was one of the most significant and influential avant-garde movements that came out of southern Europe in the late '60s. The most recognizable trait of this movement was the use of commonly found objects made of wood, metal, fabric, rocks, paper, or other leftover unknown materials that would be creatively repurposed for the artists 'use. Arte Povera formed the basis for new thinking and the beginning of a new art movement where every day became meaningful. The movement was, in some ways, a reaction against abstract painting, which dominated European art in the 50s, and was a way for artists in the movement to distinguish themselves with sculpture rather than painting.

# An Architectural Revolution

During the Depression in the 1930s, as part of Franklin Roosevelt's New Deal and the Work Progress Administration (WPA), thousands of jobs were created across the country in an effort to assist artists and architects to stimulate the economy and to provide us with steady work. The work included in that effort was to build warehouses in the least expensive way. Many of the cast-iron buildings in SoHo were part of this effort to assist workers. Most of the buildings in SoHo were manufactured with cast iron facades when they were initially built in the late 19th and early 20th centuries. The concept was to make the buildings very quickly. Using cast iron facilitated the fast build-out of these structures. Molds were used to make the facades, and the process was both quick and relatively less expensive than brick or stone. The mass production of the molds was different than the need for carving other materials by hand. The molds could be used and reused, thereby making them both cost-effective but extremely efficient as well. The strength of the iron provided the structural support that enabled the oversized windows to be used, which allowed light to flood in, as well as the high ceilings, creating large open spaces that needed only columns for support. A perfect combination of characteristics for artists 'working space.

The cast iron buildings also required frequent maintenance, by painting the facade. This needed to be done and redone more often than brick buildings. The buildings in SoHo showed different architectural designs. Some of them were reminiscent of old classic, European designs with ornamentation of European origin. Other buildings included a simple beam placed vertically or horizontally. The chaos in the design itself created harmony, which defined the beauty of that period.

The nature of New York architecture is a mix of architectural design and the freedom of architects from different periods and different styles, unlike other European cities, each of which is typically dominated by a particular design. Most buildings in SoHo have fire escapes, which are uniquely present in SoHo buildings. Those fire escapes are necessary since most warehouses in this area have only one exit, and the emergency fire escape was placed on the outside walls of the building. Some see this as beauty, while others view it as a necessary ugliness. All in all, SoHo became a landmark district, which left no room for changes, and it remains today, a part of the heritage of the New York architectural history.

In my early days residing in SoHo, it didn't have residential properties and was frequented only by workers who came during the day and left at dusk to return to wherever they came from. Only a few artists who managed to keep some of the spaces as studios remained in the neighborhood, which was deserted during the night, with all of the dirt and the chaos left behind by the workers from their day's work.

During those late hours, the streets became very quiet, dark, and unsafe. There were no street lights, and the darkness invited undesirable inhabitants who used the area for illegal activities, mainly drugs and other hazardous activities. Saying that, the artists who remained in the area were safe, and they were not harassed since we were the guardians of the darkness of SoHo.

## Being Attracted to a New Reality

SoHo had no family life. No kindergartens or schools or anything similar welcome family-oriented tenants. Artists' families chose to live elsewhere, while the artist maintained their space in SoHo as a working space only. Some of us, mainly the single people who did not have family or the means for additional space, lived in the lofts illegally, with the constant danger of being thrown out by the city or its inspectors. The area had no amenities for those of us living in SoHo, like grocery stores or other necessary services. We needed to travel many blocks just to get daily necessities. This reality was a blessing and a curse since it kept most people out of SoHo , and the few who remained enjoyed the quietness and serenity of the area.

As the trucks left at sundown, the area became empty, with no traffic of any kind. The workers went home. What was left behind was an array of empty boxes, construction debris, and other unwanted hazardous materials everywhere. Most people avoided the neighborhood, which by the dark of the night became a free-for-all all, teaming with people from all walks of life. It was scary at times as we heard gun shots out of nowhere or distant screams. Generally, nobody paid much attention since these were regular occurrences. As the early hours of dawn began to shed new life in SoHo, everything changed from the quietness to the hustle and bustle of trucks roaring, driving into warehouses to load and unload their merchandise. Life began to disturb or to add to the stimulation of the daily, chaotic, reality of SoHo. This routine brought with it the rhythm of monotonic tranquilization, which provided a stimulant of knowing what would happen in the next hour or the next day. We knew that we were safe among hard-working workers, and we knew the reasons they were there was simply to work and earn a living, and they would disappear in the evening darkness. The ones who were left behind were a small group of artists and others who were mainly residents coming from Italian backgrounds. They occupied the streets surrounding SoHo, in an area called Little Italy on one side and Chinatown on the other side, which was occupied by older people who lived there for many years in rent-controlled situations, mainly small brownstones within small apartments. As we walked through the streets in those areas, mainly after dark, you could smell the garlic of cooking by the residents or the aroma of Chinese home cooking. I found harmony in all this.

I was introduced to this lifestyle in the early days of SoHo, as I shared large spaces, lofts as we know it, with a big mattress in the center of a large, open space. There were no walls, bathrooms with no doors, and kitchens with no facility to cook except for a small hot plate. That was the reality which was reminiscent of a hard life. At the same time, the beauty of spaciousness and the freedom to run from one place to another within your living space was very attractive. We did not have much light in those empty spaces, except for large oversized windows. It was very difficult to heat these spaces due to the drafts from the large windows and the gaps in the window sills. Needless to say, we enjoyed the large windows, which in certain buildings gave us great light, either from the sky lights or from the window itself, since SoHo did not have high-rise buildings.

The infusion of light gave us the feeling of working outside in nature, in this case, an urban reality. Most lofts had exposed bricks, which added to the rustic beauty of the space. Some of them were made out of concrete floors, but the majority were wooden floors, which made lots of noise and creaks as we walked or rushed through the space. Looking from the inside out through the large windows, facing the street, we watched the workers enjoying having lunch outside. Most of them sat outside on the curb or on the stairs, chatting among themselves loudly. We heard these discussions clearly perched in our lofts many floors above ground.

You might think that would be disturbing, but to the contrary, the commotion made us feel at home and less lonely in the big studio space. As it happened because the streets were not clean, nor were they being maintained by the city, and the workers did not make any effort to clean after themselves. As a result, there was lots of trash, leftover food, and other unnecessary waste strewn everywhere. Naturally, that invited all kinds of residents, including rates, mice, or others, in search of food all hours of the day. The cockroaches emerged with no fear of people and had a feast while we watched them from our loft. Some artists among us who understood the reality of cockroaches running around like maniacs, as soon as the lights were switched on, would torment the cockroaches.

## Jack Smith and his Cockroach

One such artist is Jack Smith, a very well-known artist at the time who had worked with Andy Warhol, creating short movies. Jack lived in the center of SoHo on Greene Street. He was forced to leave his space because the landlord imposed upon him twice the legal rent and blamed him for having too many cockroaches in his space. As Jack moved to his new space, which was a block away, he collected every cockroach, put them in a jar, and took them with him to his new space. It might seem extreme that anyone would do such a thing, but Jack Smith was known as an eccentric who did many things outside the norm. Jack was a performing artist who installed a small theatre in his loft, and he would perform his artwork. The work was created around himself as a body installation. He generally appeared on the stage layering all kinds of clothes from head to toe, usually items he would find in the street, which he would then incorporate into his performances. He invited everyone to come see his performances. These would start early evening, and as we all sat and waited for his performance, not knowing when he would begin. Sometimes, he would come out and perform after four hours of waiting, and sometimes, he would never start or do any performance at all. He was considered a top-performing artist. He made a few movies, some videos, and lots of drawings where he expressed his theories on life and creating art. Needless to say, he was extremely talented and well-respected among the art crowd at that time. I got to know Jack late in his life. He liked me, I suppose because of my poor English or my accent, which he found amusing. He enjoyed visiting me at my studio on Crosby Street. I did not know much about him in my earlier years in SoHo, but I saw in him a quiet man who was uniquely different from others I met at that time. Later on, when he passed away from Aids, the story went that he felt so bad that some of his friends passed away from that disease that he infected himself with the Aids virus. By doing this, he shared the pain of his friends. That was his way of showing the impossible reality of those infected with the virus.

During that period, in the mid-seventies, I was forced to leave my space, as the landlord realized that he could generate more income from the loft by leasing it to someone else. I moved to a space on Crosby and Broome street, which I shared with Robert Grovesnor. Bob, who used the space only as a working studio, needed a roommate to share the expenses, and I took over half of the loft to work and live in.

Bob was married and father to two young children, who lived a block away from the studio on Crosby street. Neither of us cared for privacy as he walked through my living space into his working space. Bob and I appreciated each other, mainly out of curiosity, since he had not met anyone from the Middle East before me, and I stood as an enigma to him. He did not know how to deal with me, but he appreciated me for being different than others he knew throughout his life. Bob was born to an established American family and was someone for me to admire and to learn new ways of communicating from. His formative influences were different from mine.

Nightlife in SoHo was limited to a few restaurants and bars. One of them in particular was Raoul's, a French bistro that served Italian dishes and great cocktails. It is located on Prince street, between Wooster and Greene. At that time, it was the mecca for most artists who could afford to go there and have a meal. Sometimes, the bartender would give us free drinks. All in all, the ambiance and the inhabitants were mostly artists, and everybody felt at ease. Some of us walked in there straight from the studio with dirty clothes covered with paint. A block from Raoul was another Italian establishment, a place called Fanelli, an Italian/American restaurant and bar with home cooking. The owner, Mike Fanelli, and his staff were extremely welcoming to the artists who could not afford to have a meal at Raoul. The place was located on Prince and Mercer street. Mike was connected to the commerce in the area. Everybody knew him, and everybody loved and respected him. He loved the artists more than the workers in the neighborhood. We could easily get free drinks and sometimes even free meals if we did not have the money to pay for it.

At that time, in the mid-seventies, there were gas shortages in New York, and there were long lines at every gas station in the city. Mike Fanelli managed to give some of us who had cars a piece of paper on which it was written that we could fill up gas in our cars without waiting in line. The other popular establishment was located on Spring Street and West Broadway and was called the Spring Street bar. It opened in 1972 and became the bar for the few but iconic well-off artists and gallerists. Specifically, this occurred during the weekends, when patrons of the arts made their way to SoHo looking for new artists while they were wining and dining at the Spring Street bar. Most galleries at that time, during the early art scene in New York, were mainly located on 57th street and or on Madison Avenue. At that point, SoHo became desirable and the place to be for most people who were looking for a different type of entertainment, or to be seen among an artistic crowd. Among the top galleries that opened in SoHo were Leo Castelli, Paula Cooper, Sonnabend, John Weber, and other high-end top galleries. Their chosen location was mainly on West Broadway.

## New Gallery New Location

As the buzz began to take place around the art world, other galleries from mid-town began to emigrate to the downtown SoHo area. The rents for the spaces were still relatively low compared to similar spaces uptown and in midtown. This migration of other galleries and private dealers turned SoHo into a destination to see and be seen, perhaps rubbing shoulders with important art personalities, and the streets of SoHo began to be filled with many visitors and tourists alike. For the artists who lived in SoHo, the weekends were annoying because we lost the sense of an artist neighborhood, and we began to look like animals in a zoo as the visitors began to guess who was an artist or a celebrity.

Needless to say, this popularity drove prices up, and we began to pay higher prices for rent, food, and other necessities. Most of us, the artists, began to feel uncomfortable and to reject the weekly visitors who were not interested in purchasing our work. They mainly wanted to see how we lived, how we struggled in our lofts, and how we changed and designed the spaces. Generally, every space looked unique since each loft had the imprint of the artist who lived there. As you walked down the road on West Broadway, you would hit Broome Bar, which was owned by Bob and Kenny. The building was built on Broome Street in 1825. It mainly served hamburgers and beer, which was the mainstay for most of us who lived in that area.

Broome bar has the flavor and buzz of the American Midwest with low prices. You felt like you were not in New York while the visitors and tourists looked for better or higher-end food and entertainment to satisfy their curiosity after traveling from uptown to the Soho area downtown. At that time in Soho, most bars and restaurants enjoyed the artists 'being there, and they occasionally gave us free drinks and a meal or two, knowing that we would return with other patrons and generate revenue to make up for this generosity.

Once we realized that SoHo had become a destination for outside visitors, a few artists decided to open a food restaurant located on Prince and Wooster Street. It was called FOOD, opened in 1971, and closed in 1974. It was originally founded by three artists, one of them being an internationally famous conceptual artist, Gordon Matta-Clarke. Different artists/chefs were invited to cook for as many people as possible. It was practically a "soup kitchen." Different artists enjoyed cooking there for free or for a small stipend. As we enjoyed a meal for next to nothing, and sat on a bench on a long community table, perhaps not as comfortable, but the joy of having a meal with your friends and with no tourists around felt like home. During these times, we were not disturbed by being interrogated about what we did, where we lived, what kind of art we did, how much our rent was, and so far and so forth. It was a known reality, and we indulged in their curiosity, hoping that it might lead to their interest in and purchase of our work. Unfortunately, they ended up not buying our work. They were only interested in the information to share with their friends at dinner parties uptown. The food establishments were not sustainable because their priority was to feed artists, not to make a big profit. Some artists, like Richard Nonas, Jean Hasting, and Susan Harris, tried to assist in this effort to sustain FOOD and keep it open, but it was simply not viable, and in the end, it closed its doors, and the space was converted to a clothing store, as was the case with many other stores mushrooming in the area. Across the street, on Prince and Wooster Streets, was a large bakery that began to supply bread of all kinds to major supermarkets all over New York City. The bakery was operating 24/7. As the trucks were loading the bread to be delivered, if you passed by late at night when no one was around except for those making the bread, they would hand out a freshly baked loaf, still warm.

My personal experience at that time was totally different from other artists I encountered. I began to make friends with people who did not speak my language and did not share my cultural background. I was happy to assimilate myself and to absorb the new lifestyle I was so hungry for. I met other artists from different countries. One in particular, Edit DeAk, I recall vividly. She had escaped from Hungary with her boyfriend/husband, Peter Grass, when it became a communist country. She travelled through Italy and settled in America illegally. Edit was a very colorful persona who was very knowledgeable about art. She created a magazine with Walter Robinson for art and artists, mainly publishing art criticism, called Art-Rite. The publication became very influential at that time. Most artists were honored to have their art reviewed in this publication. Edit and I became good friends since we were both foreign to the American way of life. We had many things in common. We shared the struggle to make it in a new way of life. When Edith left Hungary, she lost everything she owned back home. When she began her life in SoHo as an art critic, she was approached by Walter Robinson to create the magazine. At that time the magazine was offered gratis. It was printed on newspaper stock and existed for a short period of time.

## Changing the Changes

Being outsiders, as we all attended parties which took place in different lofts and on various occasions, though always mainly during the weekends. We attended those parties whether you were invited or not. They were open to all who resided in the neighborhood. There, we met other artists, some well-known and others just at the start of their careers. At the same time, there were mothers breastfeeding their babies, suggesting the freedom to do as you pleased. The freedom was contagious, and sex was another way of expressing the freedom of love.

# Tribe of One

The '70s was the period of "making love, not war" as the prevailing attitude. The freedom of sexuality between men and women, men and men, and women and women was contagious, and all were happy to engage in whatever suited them. Taking drugs was not unusual, and taking downers was the least expensive drug to enjoy. Being depressed and/or melancholic was not considered a negative thing. I tried to stay away from most drugs and alcohol since that was not something I was familiar with or had a tolerance for. I could not stay away from the sex because that was part of my macho, male persona that I grew into from my background. I understood at that time that I had to adjust myself to participate in it all so that I could be part of what was going on.

As I tried to establish myself as an artist I was beginning to stay away from Brooklyn Museum art school, where I was previously studying. I was then rubbing shoulders with artists who already had a career and began to have shows with established galleries. I was beginning to learn the craft of establishing myself as an artist by socializing with the artists Robert Grovesnor, Bill Jensen, Bob Yesuda, Richard Nonas, and others. We played ping pong in one of the large lofts. I was taken by the warmth shown to me at these times. Perhaps because I had a strong accent and my English was still very poor. Yet I played good ping pong, and they enjoyed playing against me. This gave me confidence, and I no longer felt like an outsider as I was beginning to execute my own artwork, and I was beginning to feel the recognition that I strived for. My first show was at the Warren Benedict Gallery in 1972, and I was beginning to feel the right to conduct myself as an active participant in the art scene.

My work at that time with Warren Benedict consisted of latex sculptures. The show ended up being successful, as I learned from the art critic Judith Von Baron, with whom I had a short affair later on. Having an affair between artists and critics or art dealers was a common occurrence, and it proved to be a way for it to be mutually beneficial.

In my case, I searched for new material to create with, and this was latex. This material was suitable for me since I learned to use it as I was assisting an artist who had mastered the use of it before me. I assisted the artist, Yehuda Ben-Yehuda casting the body of human size directly by using plaster. We mixed the powder with water in order to be used directly on the skin of different models from head to toe. It took a short time for the material to dry. Once it dried we removed the person from the plaster cast and let the plaster dry further to be used again, as we cast into that shape the liquid latex. The same practice was used in different factories, using other materials, such as bronze, aluminum, or other types of metals.

As a sculptor, Yehuda inserted into the cast latex a rod that was attached to a compressor which facilitated the latex to inflate and deflate at will. This gave the impression of many bodies inflating and deflating time and time again to give the impression of soldiers who fell in war or being buried, shot, or otherwise debilitated. The impact was tremendous and viewers were shocked watching the process take place. It was difficult to watch but the power of that work reminded the viewers of different experiences that they related to things that they saw in their own past. Yehuda's work, which I helped execute, was shown at OK Harris Gallery on West Broadway. That was the first opening show of the gallery. It was a very big space, and other artists who participated with similar work included Bill Stewart, and Duane Hanson. The show was very strong and created a new wave of bodywork for other artists to follow. Duane Hanson was the leader of this movement. The owner of the gallery, Ivan Karp, ran Leo Castelli gallery before opening his own gallery. There, at Leo Castelli, he discovered these artists. When Ivan opened his own gallery, the artists moved to work with him. Ivan Karp-OK Harris was among the first galleries to open on West Broadway.

As I learned, using toxic materials, such as latex and polyurethane, can be very dangerous because the fumes of these materials are deadly to breathe. I worked for three years with this material and was beginning to feel sick from it. I went to visit my doctor, and I came to realize that I could no longer work with latex. I tried to stop and think in a new direction, but the result was impossible. Therefore, destroying the work that I already succeeded to complete was the only way to start all over again with totally different material. At that time, an artist friend had a pick-up truck. We loaded on the truck all of my work made with latex and took it to the dump to be destroyed away from my frame of mind. Consequently, I was forced to search and adopt new materials and new ideas to be the basis of my thinking and my work. I began to use aluminum and wood together with my painting, which used mostly acrylics.

## I Think Therefore I Am

The art scene movement in the 70's was between conceptual and minimal art. I wanted to be part of that movement and I began to think similarly and created art accordingly, to find my place in time and in those categories. The lack of fluidity in the language limited me to be able to excel in that direction since both of those categories required articulation of your doing. Therefore, my art spoke to transmit my ideas, not through the spoken but rather through physical activity. Some other artists learned, soon enough, that conceptual art and minimal art were very difficult to make a living from this art form. For those artists doing this kind of work and not being able to earn a living from it, they turned to other professions in order to make a living. Some of us worked as waiters while others as plumbers and electricians, even though none of us knew how to do it legally. At that time, most renovations in SoHo lofts were illegally done and not according to any code. The inspectors and the authorities did not believe that we were going to stay for long, so they were dismissive and did not bother to check if we had the license to do this work. That practice conceived in the early days continued for years as we renovated our own places and other places as well.

Life in SoHo at this time was hard in some ways and in other ways, easy since we did need any wealth to enjoy life. It was easy to survive, and we helped each other, and on occasion, we received free drinks, mainly in the late night as we strolled from one bar to another. The patrons of these places were happy to see us as we were the local residents, and we became a desirable community. As a side benefit, we drew others to their establishments. As the tourists were seeking something new and different, they would come to SoHo in the early evenings, and they would return to where they came from. We remained sitting on the stools at the bar. We would exchange ideas or perhaps gossip about who was managing to succeed and who failed in their pursuit of recognition. We made fun of each other to air out our frustrations, and in the end, we all went home to our large lofts. Some of us started working while others fell asleep, either drunk or having overused alcohol.

Consciously, we all tried to succeed in a sea of ideas that took place between our conscious and subconscious reality, which brought upon us a sense of melancholy. Some of us took it with ease, while others suffered tremendously from this internal dialogue.

I think, therefore I am, Descartes 'description of self and consciousness continues to be defined by Hegel as a consciousness that attains its satisfaction by the self-consciousness of another. He argued only in the relationship to and the recognition of/by the other it exists and manifests itself from a desire to actual self-awareness. This dialectic argument that consciousness stems from the individual and reflects the self in the eye of the other reaches far into the 20th century and into psychoanalysis from Freud to Lacan to Irigaray. Or in other words, self-consciousness is defined as a dialectic between at least two, the own self and the other. It was turned around and reinterpreted by Karl Marx, who gave this relationship a wider, larger perspective with the observation that consciousness by itself does not define or shape our decisions, but that consciousness itself depends on our circumstances of being and that our consciousness is formed by our experiences and the circumstances we live in.

# Anne – the French

My mother, as a young widow in a foreign country where she didn't speak the language, became very lonely. This was exacerbated when most of her children left our family home, one after the other, to start their own families. In Iraq, she had married from a very young age. There was very little left of her support network now, and this isolated her and drove her to want to establish a social network outside of our home. I felt the duty of wanting to comfort her and give her the companionship she craved. Our inability to communicate made this difficult, her not speaking Hebrew, and my losing the Arabic I had spoken in my early years. Our interactions were limited to small exchanges with our eyes or body language. She felt helpless as a parent to me, only able to provide my most basic needs, like cooking dinner and keeping our home clean. I, in turn, did not have the means or knowledge to support her and help her escape her lonely reality.

We were codependent, and yet, with limited ability to provide what the other needed. My mother lived alone in our family home, outside of Tel Aviv, and would busy herself with going to the grocery store to shop for our needs. On one of these trips, she met a man who took an interest in her and eventually mustered the confidence to approach her. This was the first time she had engaged with anyone from outside of our immediate family since leaving Iraq. Eventually, this budding friendship developed to where he was walking her home from the store on a regular basis. He also was an older French immigrant and did not speak the local language either. This meant no verbal communication, yet again, and created a friendship akin to what she shared with me, based on gestures and facial expressions.

At that time, telephones were still a novelty, and only the richest had access to one. It was commonplace for people to just stop by when they wanted to connect with one another. My mother's new friend started to stop by our home regularly, and this pleased my mother very much. They would sit together on the front staircase, not saying much. She would make him tea, and they would share whatever stories they were able to. By the end of the day, he would return to his empty home, and they both would eagerly await the next day when they would repeat this ritual. This man was of French origin and eventually suggested to my mother that he teach me French. This pleased my mother very much. This was an additional reason for him to spend more time with my mother without there being any other intention. In our culture, it was not acceptable for a woman like my mother to have male friends. Having a reason for him to visit our home must have given her tremendous peace of mind.

I was a teenager at this time, and to please my mother, I accepted the French lessons from this stranger. I was proud of the fact that I had found a way to support my mother and help ease her pain. I never did learn enough from him, as I did not appreciate this opportunity at the time, but I was very happy to see them together. This started my love affair and affection for the French language, as it until this day, remains linked to my fondest memories of my mother.

Traveling back and forth between NYC, Israel, and Europe, mainly Paris, I began to expand my French vocabulary. This enhanced my ability to communicate in French, and to engage with the locals on those visits. During that period, in the late seventies, I had an art exhibit in Switzerland, close to Geneve. I connected in London on my return from Geneve to NYC, and as I was standing in the check-in line at Heathrow airport when, a young French woman tapped me on the shoulder, asking whether that was the correct line for the flight to New York. This started an extended conversation.

# Tribe of One

We were both on the same flight to New York and when we got to the front of the ticket line, the person at the counter assumed we were a couple and seated us together on the flight.

Seated next to one another, the conversation flowed freely, and we came to learn a lot about one another. Anne was young, barely 19, and beautiful. I was in my mid-thirties, and I felt significantly older. I learned that she was a dancer, and told her about my life as an artist. We kept talking and discovering more intimate details about one another. I liked her right away. Not only was she beautiful, but also very entertaining and intelligent. Anne seemed to be fascinated by me, the first artist she had ever met, and she confided in me in more ways than one. I had never met a professional dancer either, and Anne explained that she was flying to New York to join the dance company of the then-famed Jennifer Miller.

Anne had the grace of a dancer, and I felt her hunger for the promise of a world with endless possibilities. It was not only her physique but also her personality that was very attractive to me. She seemed mature for her age and knew far more of the world than I had until then. She was confident and open to what the future might bring. Her radiant excitement was contagious, and so was her almost insatiable curiosity about all new experiences and encounters, including this one with me.

We communicated well, she with her French-accented English and its charming imperfections, and me, with my limited vocabulary and confidence in English. Our communication was improved, in all the other ways we could interact. As soon as we were seated and before the plane had taken off, we started kissing. This continued through the remainder of the flight to NYC. It was the proverbial Love at First Sight. During the flight, I learned that Anne needed a place to live upon arrival on American soil. She had a few addresses in NYC where she could stay with friends, or rather friends of friends until she found an apartment. I immediately offered that she could stay with me instead, and she accepted without hesitation and continued flirting with me.

Our romance started on British Airways and continued in the studio I shared with Bob Grosvenor on Broome and Crosby Streets. Anne was excited by the prospect of living in a loft in SoHo, in the heart of the dance and art worlds. My excitement matched hers. She needed a place to stay and someone to show her the city, and I was looking for a love affair. We developed a strong trust in each other almost immediately, despite our differing backgrounds and the age gap.

Anne had very little time in New York before she was to join Jennifer Miller's dance company, and so we spent her first day together in SoHo. I was happy and proud to show her the city that had become my home. Before coming to New York, Anne had often been to Japan for modeling engagements and only knew New York from layovers. That first evening, I took her out to dinner and introduced her to my friend, John Giordano, whom I had met at the art school of the Brooklyn Museum. I was proud to introduce my friends to Anne, even though we had just met, and they, in turn, were immediately smitten by her, which made me feel even more at ease with her and with our strange situation. This was only our first day together.

The next day, Anne went to register with Jennifer Miller Dance Company and I accompanied her and got to meet Jennifer, who I found to be the most interesting Southern woman. Anne also took dance classes with the Merce Cunningham Dance Company. It was a tremendous achievement to have been accepted as a professional dancer or student with both of those companies in their prime. Anne was dancing all day and late into the night.

Being a young dancer was very different from being an artist. It required many hours of daily rigorous physical training and intense maintenance of the body. I, on the other hand, was in my studio working, quite solitarily, or socializing with my friends, and by the time Anne arrived at the loft, we were both exhausted from our separate demanding schedules, leaving us with very little time or energy for each other. In these late nights, we were too tired to do much, whether connecting just the two of us, or socializing with the outside world.

Apart from separately engaging in what we each loved to do, we needed to earn a living, and we each made very little money. There was a fascination with each other's struggles to make it in a foreign country and in a city like New York, juggling all these conflicting priorities. Together, we lived rather modestly, and what kept us going was, to a large degree our mutual fascination with one another.

In my case, I could impress my artist friends with a youthful and talented dancer girlfriend, something that I savored. Our circumstances triggered in me the desire to guide and protect her. With Anne, I had the opportunity to meet a lot of dancers and realized that they were a breed of their own. Their physicality and maintaining this was all that consumed their days, improving on it every day by exercising and shaping it further. As an artist, and especially at that time, exercise was not a priority for me. My physicality was directed towards the creation and struggle to produce my work.

Anne and I managed to live on a meager budget and were still able to enjoy the indulgences our hearts desired. Anne came from a modest and humble home. She knew exactly how and where to cut costs in our spending, and I, in turn, came from an even less affluent background. Between the two of us, we managed to indulge in the foods and experiences we cared for, despite our limited means.

Our social life revolved around her fellow dancers and was easily intertwined with my friends from the art world. Although those two categories of artists did not overlap much and had no cognition of one another, when it came to socializing and partying, they seemed to share common grounds.

Jennifer Miller knew how to surround herself with lively people who loved to drink, dance, and be merry. Boredom was not something that anyone suffered from in those circles. Jennifer, at times would be sad or anxious, but this never revealed itself in her work or at her parties. In one of her pieces, Lovers, the sadness and beauty were overwhelming, and the melancholy finally closed with a happy ending, raising the work's mood.

Jennifer, loved and revered by much of the dance community in NYC, was a successful choreographer and was regularly invited to perform with her company across Europe and Latin America. I learned that being a dancer is far harder than being an artist. I could work from my studio day in and day out, whereas Anne needed the flexibility and physical strength to sustain the rigor required in the choreography of their dances. A lot of jealousy and backstabbing occurred amongst the dancers, particularly who was in or out or who received a government grant to continue their work. Most dancers were not paid for anything other than the actual performances, and this was only a fraction of what they needed to survive. This resulted in a lot of mental anguish for the dancers, and needless to say, the physical demands only exacerbated these pressures. In order to maintain their strength and flexibility, the dancers invested a lot of time in exercise, massage, and other costly endeavors. Sustaining the body and mind is the highest priority for dancers, and achieving this tranquility is extremely difficult.

Sometime in that first year with the Jennifer Muller Company, Anne was invited to perform in South America and was the only non-American in the group. They went on to perform across multiple countries and were gone for a month or longer. Upon the Company's return to NYC, Anne realized that she didn't have the correct US visa to be allowed back into the country. She was stranded in Argentina.

I did everything I could to help her return to NYC, but as far as the immigration authorities were concerned, there was no proof that she had legitimate grounds for returning. In an effort to prove this, I turned to an immigration lawyer friend, Allen Kay, and through him, we initiated a procedure to bring her back home to me in NYC.

A year into our relationship, we each started to realize the hardship of our situation and our limited abilities to support one another, particularly financially. We began to understand that we each needed more than the other could provide. As we were in different industries, we kept at it, attempting to make things work, but as time went on, this proved futile. Anne needed more attention and support as a young dancer in NYC, and I was less and less able to maintain an interest in her group of young dancers. She, in turn, was not able to support me in my work, or understand my more mature challenges. We started to drift apart and tried to find the support we each needed outside of the relationship.

I continued to pursue my career in the cutthroat and closed art world amongst the Ivy League-educated artists. Anne also began to realize that her career as a dancer was best served by her return to France, her home country, where she could create her own dance company.

Without the required immigration status, Anne could not establish a sustainable career in NYC. She could not qualify for government grants to support her work in the US, and even as a dancer in other companies, she was not able to receive payment for her work. She survived the years on her limited savings and whatever her parents could periodically send to support her.

I could barely earn enough money, and yet we managed to maintain a decent lifestyle. Despite us trying to make the most of our time together, two years into our relationship, Anne moved out of my loft on Crosby Street and rented her own shabby little apartment blocks away on Elizabeth Street. I helped her settle into this new life, helping paint the rooms and find furniture. This was the beginning of our separation as lovers, but it did not stop us from remaining close confidants, having recognized that we needed one another, if only as supportive friends.

Soon after Anne became comfortable being in her surroundings back in Paris and began to make new friends, she met Bernard Bousquet. Bernard was a psychiatrist, as well. He was also an artist and painted large-scale paintings. The two fell in love, and Bernard began to help Anne with the scenery and stage design for her performances. The two enjoyed working together, fell in love, and got married. They started a company together, Le Generateur, which became one of the most important outlets for performance art in Paris. Many artists from all over the world chose to and enjoyed performing there. Anne with Bernard established themselves as a major force in the performing art scene in Paris.

We remained in close contact, despite the distance between us, and supported one another in our new endeavors and personal relationships with other men and women. We came to the realization that we are one another's emotional support, but needed, in addition to this, the patronage of our community to continue to create, and thrive in our respective fields.

# The End of One

As my life drifted away from a relationship with Anne Dreyfus, I found myself again in a situation of bachelorhood. I attended a few parties that led me nowhere, looking around, perhaps for something to do or someone to share my life with. It was hard for me to maintain life by myself. I feared being alone in this city where I had not totally acclimated. I was used to a life in which the communal aspect prevailed and made me feel a sense of belonging. The life that I left was easy to inhabit and was one to which I was accustomed and suited my personality.

Relocating to the United States was not only difficult but also required adapting, both culturally and financially, the pressure of which impacted my mental well-being. Earning a living in a city in which I did not know anyone was a hard task.

It happened that one evening, as I was working in my studio, not particularly stimulated and feeling averse to being alone, I received a call from a friend who asked me to join him at a party to which he was invited. I instinctively declined the invitation as it had not been extended to me personally by the host, and I was proud. My friend insisted that I join, so I ended up going to the party, which turned out to be quite boring. Yet, this was where I met a striking woman. I first noticed her big blue eyes resting on my face, probably wondering who I was or why I was there. Maybe she could tell from looking at me that I felt lost or out of place. I tried to impress her by inviting her to dance with me. I kept her on the dance floor for as long as I could. It was my way of commanding her time and attention at the party without being self-conscious of the fact that I did not know anyone else in the room.

The party went on, and I found myself walking home alone, wondering why did I not ask for her phone number. As my regrets dawned on me, without believing in fate, I said to myself, maybe my error was fate, as I was still in a relationship with Anne Dreyfus at the time.

Many weeks later, over lunch at a small coffee shop in Tribeca, to my surprise, two attractive young women walk in. One of them looked at me and asked if I remembered her. Of course, I remembered her, the woman I had danced the night away with weeks prior. Perhaps I wanted to see her again, and now that she stood in front of me, I immediately asked for her number. I was not going to repeat the mistake twice. Since I was about to travel abroad, I told her I would call her when I returned from my trip. It seemed to me that she was happy about that and was willing to meet with me again. I did not have anyone to share my life with at that time.

When I returned, I called her, and I was happy that she accepted my invitation to my studio on Crosby Street for dinner. I promised to cook. By that point I knew how to cook pretty well, since my life required that I learn to cook for myself. We shared a beautiful evening, and I learned quite a bit about her. I learned that her name was Helaine Funk, and she went by Lani. She began to share her background with me. The conversation went well. In an attempt to satisfy my curiosity about this graceful creature, the evening's conversation revolved around her. I loved to hear her speak and watch her facial expressions.

Sitting across from her, I could not fathom what she may find interesting about me. Nothing of my story felt impressive to me. Needless to say, where most of my relationships to date were largely limited to sexual attraction, with Lani, something was different. I felt perhaps that this was someone who I could have a fuller existence with, and dare I imagine, a sustainable relationship.

Lani was very open and willing to absorb my complexities. I began to to build a self-awareness of the challenges presented by some aspects of my personality. I was taken by her empathy and appreciation and felt more drawn to Lani than anyone I had been involved with to date. I felt that she could help and support me and that I could reciprocate, as she understood my need to share and to explore the downtown SoHo area.

In those early days of the relationship, not many would be willing to move to SoHo, out of fear of crime or out of a loss of community. Later on, I learned that was what impressed Lani. At that time, Lani lived uptown, and downtown was an enigma for her. She realized that I needed someone to share my space with, and it did not take long to decide to move into my studio. Perhaps a shabby loft in SoHo, too big to control, too dirty to keep clean with high ceilings, which made one feel a bit lost, in hindsight, seems to have impressed her most.

Lani grew up in a middle-class lifestyle, attending proper schools, and it was finally her moment to stray freely and discover something very different. I felt that her willingness to accept all of what was my life at the time might just be what I needed in the person to adopt into my world and share with unconditionally and without judgment. Perhaps this suited me since, in my background, relationships were the highest priority, and a proper home was important to me, especially after having endured years of life in chaos.

I learned from my father that law and order within a person is important. I lived with this in mind all through my life. My father, who was born and lived in Iraq under British rule, was accustomed to and lived a very ordered life. He was never a soldier, but he was predisposed to live his life as a soldier under the command of orderliness.

# Epilogue

Most people ask artists why they do what they do when there is not a financial reward. When the fame is both hard to achieve, regularly coupled with much heartbreak, and at a usually steep reality. I have not found an answer to this question, as I myself have not figured out why I became an artist.

Most of us don't know what we want to become. Only a few amongst us can claim to know what we want to be from a young age. My choice continues to be a mystery to me today, just as it has been throughout my life. I only feel good when an artwork is completed, knowing that the next piece will be better than what I just created.

I am regularly ambivalent about the work I am creating, and perhaps that is the source of my drive and what keeps me wanting to try again and again. To complete my vision for work is to set it free in the world so it may create its own existence, not necessarily limited or formed by my initial concept of it. More than lines on a page, the value of an artwork is in its appreciation and recognition, whether by the art world or people in general.

I attempted to summarize my life as an artist. I do not regret attempting to become an artist, but I am happy for those who did not choose this path for themselves. Saying this, I cannot imagine doing anything else myself. The struggle to create and to keep building myself as I look toward my next endeavor is my life's pursuit.

# Tribe of One

# Tribe of One

# Tribe of One

# Tribe of One

# Tribe of One

Made in the USA
Columbia, SC
14 November 2024